Revisiting Gender and Migration

TRANSNATIONAL PRESS LONDON

Books by TPL

Revisiting Gender and Migration

Market Efficiency and Long-run Price Leadership in the US Energy Market

Transferring Procedural Knowledge from Multinationals to Local Distributors in Saudi Arabia

International Operations, Innovation and Sustainability

Overeducated and Over Here

Image of Istanbul: Impact of ECOC 2010 on the city image

Women from North Move to South: Turkey's Female Movers from the Former Soviet Union Countries

Turkish Migration Policy

Conflict, Insecurity, and Mobility

Family and Human Capital in Turkish Migration

Little Turkey in Great Britain

Politics and Law in Turkish Migration

Turkish Migration, Identity and Integration

Journals by TPL

Migration Letters

Remittances Review

Göç Dergisi

Border Crossing

Journal of Gypsy Studies

Kurdish Studies

Transnational Marketing Journal

Revisiting Gender and Migration

Edited by

M. Murat Yüceşahin

Pınar Yazgan

TRANSNATIONAL PRESS LONDON

2017

Revisiting Gender and Migration

Edited by M. Murat Yüceşahin and Pınar Yazgan

First Published in 2017 by TRANSNATIONAL PRESS LONDON in the United Kingdom, 12 Ridgeway Gardens, London, N6 5XR, UK.
www.tplondon.com

Hardcover

ISBN: 978-1-910781-61-6

Cover Design: Gizem Çakır

www.tplondon.com

Contents

Acknowledgements

As the editors, we particularly thank all the contributors of this volume. We thank to Saniye Dedeoğlu for her contribution in review and early preparation stages of this edited volume. We thank Nirmala Arunasalam for her comments and editorial help in preparation of the manuscript. We also thank all the colleagues who reviewed the earlier versions of the selected chapters prior to publication.

About the Contributors

Professor Victor Agadjanian (PhD University of Southern California; Foundation Distinguished Professor) conducts research on various aspects of social and demographic change in developing and transitional settings. He has studied migration, sexual and reproductive behavior, gender, ethnicity, and religion. He has directed several large projects funded by the National Institutes of Health, United States Agency for International Development, and other agencies in sub-Saharan Africa and Central Eurasia (Russia, the Caucasus, and Central Asia). He has published in several languages in leading international scholarly outlets.

Gül İnce Beqo is currently completing her double PhD at Università Cattolica del Sacro Cuore di Milano and Regent's University, London in Sociology, Organization and Culture, with a specialization in migration and family studies. In Turkey she graduated from the Pamukkale University with a Bachelor of Arts in Sociology in 2006. She completed her Master's degree in Communication Sciences (Radio, TV and Cinema) at Ege University. In 2007 she moved to Italy and graduated from the Eastern Piedmont University in Modern Foreign Languages (Spanish-English). She is the winner of VIII edition of the Italian National Literary Competition "Lingua Madre", promoted by the Women Thoughts Studies Centre and the first to be dedicated to foreign women living in Italy. She is also an Italian-Spanish-English sworn translator and interpreter.

Dr Emel Coşkun is Assistant Professor of Sociology at Duzce University, Turkey. She received her PhD in Migration Studies at the University of Kent in 2013. Her research interests relate to gender and migration fields including undocumented women migrants in labour markets, migration politics, prostitution regimes, human trafficking. Her recent articles focus on sex trafficking and undocumented women migrants' experiences in Turkey. Her current focus is on asylum seeker/refugee women's experiences in Turkey and social work.

Dr Sevim Atila Demir is Associate Professor in the Department of Sociology at Sakarya University, Sakarya, Turkey. She graduated from Department of Sociology at Dumlupinar University, in 2004. She obtained her master's degree with a thesis titled "Effect of Social Change on Family and Old People (A research of five retirement house in Istanbul" in 2006 at Sakarya University and her PhD thesis was titled "Divorce among Turkish

Migrant Families : the case of Germany" submitted in 2010 at the same University. Her research interests include family sociology, gender studies, migration and elderly people on which she has published several articles.

Dr Roel Jennissen is researcher at the Netherlands Scientific Council for Government Policy (WRR). He obtained a PhD in demography from the University of Groningen on the basis of the book *Macro-Economic Determinants of International Migration in Europe* (2004). Currently, his main research interests are crime, international migration and super-diversity.

Dr Işık Kulu-Glasgow is a researcher at the Research and Documentation Centre (WODC) of the Dutch Ministry of Security and Justice. She has been involved in different research projects on asylum, migration and integration. Her research interests include immigration policy, marriage migration, labour migration, and integration of migrants.

Dr Monika Smit heads the research division Administration of Justice, Legislations and International and Aliens Affairs (RWI) of the Research and Documentation Centre (WODC) at the Ministry of Security and Justice in the Netherlands. Before that she worked among others, as a senior researcher at the Bureau of the Dutch national rapporteur on trafficking in human beings (2000-2009) and as an assistant professor Child and Youth Care at Leiden University (1983-2000).

Dr Pelin Sönmez completed her BA in Political Sciences and International Relations Department in the Faculty of Economics and Administrative Sciences at Başkent University, Ankara in 2002. Then, she continued with her MA degree in European Union in the Graduate School of Social Sciences at Dokuz Eylül University. She received her PhD in the same field of her MA in the Graduate School of Social Sciences at Istanbul University in 2014. Since she became PhD, she has been working in the Department of International Relations at Nişantaşı University. She wrote chapters for several books like "Europe Seen Here and Elsewhere: Eurobroadmap Visions of Europe in the World", "The Expansion of EU in Eastern Europe and Western Balkans: Is EU 36 Possible?", "European Union and Member States: A Research on EU 15."In addition to these works, she published several articles in different academic journals, such as Ankara European Studies, Social Sciences Journal of Dokuz Eylül University, Journal of the Black Sea Studies, and Migration Journal. She is still working on European Union, the relationship between Turkey and EU, political integration, migration policies.

Dr Pınar Yazgan is Assistant Professor of Sociology at Sakarya University, Turkey. She received her BA, MA and PhD in Sociology, all from Sakarya University Her PhD research focused on the sense of identity and belonging amongst migrants from Turkey in Denmark, and she is also a research grant recipient from the Scientific and Technological Research Council of Turkey. She conducted field work in Denmark between 2007 and 2009 while also serving as a visiting researcher at the Danish National Research Centre for Social Sciences. Her recent research focuses on the integration of different generations of migrants from Turkey in Drammen, Norway. Her research interests include transnationalism, mobility, gender and critical discourse analysis with a special focus on migrants. Dr Yazgan is Book Review Editor of *Migration Letters*. She is also one of the editors of *Göç Dergisi* (Migration Journal) and regular contributor of The Migration Conferences.

Dr M. Murat Yüceşahin is Associate Professor at Ankara University, Faculty of Language and History-Geography, Department of Geography, Turkey. After received his PhD from the Institute of Social Sciences at Ankara University in 2002, Dr Yüceşahin's major research area is population geography. In 2011, as a collaborator researcher, Dr. Yüceşahin participated to the World Population Programme at the International Institute for Applied Systems Analysis (IIASA), Laxenburg, Austria and worked on Turkey's fertility, mortality and migration trends and sub national level population projection. His current research primarily focuses on feminist geography, population geography, and urban social geography. In addition to his many currently academic works, Dr. Yüceşahin is managing editor of *Göç Dergisi* (Migration Journal).

Natalia Zotova is PhD candidate at the Ohio State University. She is a cultural anthropologist who studies Central Asian migration to the U.S. and Russia, and its health outcomes. She conducted research among Central Asian migrants in various regions of Russia and Central Asia (Tajikistan, Kyrgyzstan). Natalia Zotova explores experiences of migrants, resources and social networks that they use while accommodating to a new setting, as well as perceptions of stress and insecurity. Natalia aims to conceptualize complex relationships of Central Asian migrants with the new social environment, when they re-develop their empirical, existential and social selves in the place of destination. She is also interested in the implications of transnational migration for the physical and psychological well-being of movers.

Chapter One

Introduction: Revisiting Gender in the Context of Migration

Pınar Yazgan and **M. Murat Yüceşahin**

Gender in migration studies, we believe, is linked to feminist studies in the broader sense. The concept of feminism comes from the term "womanism" and was first used in the 1890s. It is used as a general label for women's movements and the struggle for equal rights for women. Whilst it reflects a wide range of definitions, its purpose is to create awareness on the secondary status of women compared to men. It also examines the associated discrimination imposed on woman through culture and religion. This discrimination produces unequal power relations between men and women. In a broad sense, feminism is an act that aims to rearrange the world on the basis of gender equality in all forms of human relations and to act against gender-based discrimination. The movement seeks to neutralise gender based bias and declare a world with equal rights for all by virtue of their common humanity (Tilly and Gurin, 1990: 20).

Feminism aims to emancipate women from social, political and ideological bias. Gender-based cultural values, habits and practices which have been built into societies sustain power, privilege and domination of men. This tries to reverse the perception that women are reflected as invisible, dependent and passive. Gender roles provide difficulties for men and woman alike. However, the severity of these difficulties is more prevalent in woman (Slattery, 2015: 137-145).

Feminism pushes the academia rethink perceptions which portray women as invisible and weak. Within feminism, there has been a broad theoretical perspective which addresses the different causes of inequality, patriarchy and gender differences and which suggests different solutions against all of these. Patriarchy describes the dominance of men in its many physical, political, and ideological guises. As a result, the concept is prevalent in feminist analysis and Walby (1996) adds these to key feminist concepts. However, there is no consensus on the conceptualization of the various theories, for example patriarchal theory is based on feminism.

The feminist critique has found two places in migration literature. Anthias and Yuval-Davis (1983: 62) point out that "Black, minority and migrant women have been on the whole invisible within the feminist movement in Britain and within the literature on women's or feminist studies." Their paper argues over the issue of interrelationship of ethnic and gender divisions and claims that the 'ethnic' context of feminist struggles is a neglected area. It has led to an analysis of these black women's experience of migration. In 2008, Castles and Miller also outline that the position of women constitutes as not only sex but also class, race, ethnicity and sexual orientation. Thus, migration is a sexist field and subject.

International migration refers to the important links between class, ethnicity and gender, as well as identifying labour market patterns. The role of women in providing new workers for the country of their origin was very important in terms of the economic benefits of labour migration. The rate of migrant female workers was large. Attributing a low status to immigrant female workers was partly easy as a patriarchal society assigns the women's primary role as mother and wife. For this reason they are paid less than men. In this regard, immigrant women's work experiences are often different from men's experiences. Women are generally concentrated in repetitive task occupations and in personal or community services, such as factory jobs, low-skilled jobs and traditional care roles. In recent years, with the decline of the manufacturing sector, there has been a partial shift towards white-collar jobs. Further, immigrant women generally are not reflected on statistics because of their dependent status (Walby, 2007; Giddens and Sutton, 2014: 197).

The rapid political and social changes in today's world have severe effects on human mobility. There are about 250 million international migrants constituting almost 3.4 per cent of the world's population, and about half of them are women (Sirkeci, 2017: 129). Among migrant women, there are migrant workers, refugees, and displaced and trafficked people (Jolly *et al.*, 2005). Thus, migration has become an increasingly important issue due to its effects in different areas, and the position of women in the migratory processes. Migration may have a role in changing gender norms which, in certain circumstances, can constitute a barrier for women to gain access to education and economic opportunities. However, it may also provide more equitable social norms which can improve women's rights and access to resources. Migrant women either return home or settle in a new country and maintain their newfound autonomy, bringing with them new norms, skills and expertise. It can increase gender discrimination and violence whilst supporting or creating sex-segregated legal or illegal markets with undocumented domestic workers and trafficking of people. Hence, migration has both benefits and risks from the gender perspective.

Ravenstein (1885) can be considered as the pioneer who had analysed the gender effects on migration, referring to both internal and international moves. This formed a basis for following development of feminist analysis, which dates back to the beginning of the 1970s (Brettell, 2016: 1). In 1984, Thadani and Todaro (1984) published a paper in which they point out gender-related differences in migration and the need for an analysis of female migration, offering a gender-specific framework and a model. They claimed that their contemporary research drew attention to the expanding stream of female migration and the problem of analysing female migration and its difficulties. In 1991, Bonney and Love (1991) published a paper in which they described the findings from a survey of migrants arriving in Aberdeen in 1986. Their research findings reflected the perception that migrant wives' roles are orientated beginning with their husbands' occupational concerns. However, this need not determine their labour market activity. Chant (1992) points out the need for a model of female migration, raises concern over deficiencies in major theoretical approach and claims that gender inequality, inequality to access to jobs and low-income populations are major policy issues. Shildrick's (1997) book, entitled *Leaky bodies and boundaries: Feminism, postmodernism and (bio) ethics*, suggests a postmodern feminist analysis of bioethics and analyses the concepts of women, bodies and ethics. The editor of *Gender and Migration*, Sweetman (1998), argues that gender analysis is a fundamental tool in studying migration and claims that migration is part of a livelihood strategy, of a family where human existence depends not only on production but reproduction. In 2006, a case study entitled *Queer intersections: Sexuality and gender in migration studies* analysed Filipina migrant workers and the historical and theoretical development of sexuality in migration research (Manalansan, 2006).

Recent developments in women's studies have led to a renewed interest in gender studies; nevertheless, these changes are having an effect and a need, which represent different theoretical and analytical tools rather than sex as a dichotomous variable. There is increasing concern about using theoretical approaches of gender as relational, spatially and contextually (Piper, 2005:1). Therefore, gender is an increasingly important concept in different areas as an analytical tool and research lens to understand how societies function, depending on diversified theoretical orientations. The literature on gender has mainly focused on gender identity, gendered representations, gender roles, gender politics, femininity and masculinity (e.g. Blom, 1999; Gerson, 2004; Piper, 2005; Donato *et al.*, 2006). West and Zimmerman (1987:126) state that analysing gender involves socially guided perceptual, interactional and micro-political activities that cast particular pursuits as expressions of masculine and feminine "natures".

The role of gender in the contemporary world is at the heart of understanding migration studies. Recent developments in human mobility have heightened the need for bringing gendered approaches to all aspects of the issues of conflict and movement regarding states, societies and families from broadening perspectives to the accurate understanding of the whole process (Sirkeci *et al.*, 2012; Brettell, 2016; Massey, 2015). Migration has been identified as the significant contributing factor for the rise of gender role awareness and building human capital (Milewski *et al.*, 2015; Fleury, 2016).

Chapters in this book cover the refugee crisis, family, marriage, undocumented migration to sexual exploitation from the gender perspective. In these chapters questions have been raised about the different effects of migration on gender norms and social life for women. Thus, they provide the overview of studies on gender perspective that comprise case studies of migration research on gender in Germany, Russia, the Netherlands, Turkey and Italy. This is to highlight major theoretical developments relating to gender relations, migration policy, family, marriage, legislation, labour and sexual exploitation.

The chapters also discuss performativity, representation, marriage, Central Asian migration, gender specific segmented labour markets, legislation, Labour, sexual Exploitation, family perspective in migration, social capital and Syrian refugee crisis and gender policies in host societies through a gendered lens. This is to raise some questions on the future impact of the gender issues and approaches on the scope and scale of this human mobility for future research.

Migration is an inclusive process and therefore deserves a comprehensive approach. Complex relations in terms of gender relations and practices and how they mutually interact and reproduce social spaces are examined. Geographical analyses of migration examine gender differences most centrally in terms of space and power. More specifically, feminist geographers have developed insight into the gender dimensions of the social construction of scale, the socio-spatial (re)production in relation to gender roles and practices. In *Deconstructing the Gender-Migration Relationship: Performativity and Representation*, Murat Yüceşahin introduces a theoretical spatial approach in order to reach a resolution in the gender-migration relationship. First, Yüceşahin reviews gender practices of the migrating households in the scope of performative patriarchal power relations, and then addresses the relationship between gender, migration and economic reconstruction in transnational spaces. Finally, this paper enables us to resolve the interactive transformation of gender, international migration and urbanization processes within the scope of reproduction of transnational social spaces.

Central Asian migrants find their way around in new countries, work and study, have families, become permanent residents or eventually return home. While settling in their countries of destination, these migrants redefine their cultural values and renegotiate gender roles in the new context. Natalia Zotova's paper entitled *Gendered Pathways: Central Asian Migration through the Lens of Embodiment* discusses transnational migration from Central Asia and employs the framework of embodiment to address subjective experiences of migrants. It also conceptualizes migrants' existential experiences in the places of destination, and their complex relationships with the new social environment. Further, it also outlines how migrants re-develop their empirical, existential and social selves while settling in destination countries, such as Russia and the US. The phenomenological framework of this paper helps us to understand transnational migration as dynamically embodied action. Furthermore, it allows addresses gendered responses to transnational migration, and their implications for the physical and psychological well-being of Central Asian migrants in the new destinations.

Sham marriages are established with the sole aim of obtaining a residence permit. Using evidence from the literature, data from population registers, archive research at the immigration office and interviews, Kulu-Glasgow, Smit and Jennissen's paper, entitled *For Love or for Papers? Sham Marriages among Turkish (Potential) Migrants and Their Gender Implications*, focuses on the prevalence and forms of manifestation of Turkish sham marriages in the Netherlands. They present narratives of different forms of manifestation and analyse the gender impacts of different sham marriages. Their findings indicate that most Turkish migration marriages are genuine and that often women act as active agents in bilateral constructions of commercial sham marriages. They are sponsors or intermediaries in criminal networks or private spheres and sometimes seek a fake groom for money to secure a residence permit themselves. Sometimes they themselves are victims of bilateral sham marriages as they do not receive the money they were promised for acting as a fake bride. In cases of unilateral sham marriages female sponsors are victims, as they think that the relationship is for love and not for papers.

Women migrants have been visible in gender-specific segmented labour markets of Turkey since the early 1990s. Although the forms of women's migration and ethnicity diversified in the last decades, their undocumented position has remained and led to differences between men in the informal working and living conditions. Based on existing literature and research, Emel Coşkun's paper, entitled *Undocumented Migrant Women in Turkey: Legislation, Labour and Sexual Exploitation*, analyses undocumented migrant women's position in Turkey's migration regime by focusing on legislation on migration, labour market and prostitution regimes. It is argued that Turkey's current migration and labour regimes structurally create vulnerabilities for migrant women, as they are pushed to work in gendered segments of the labour market informally and in the most precarious positions. These vulnerabilities facilitate the way for labour exploitation and result in gendered risks, such as sexual harassment or being pushed to sell sex. This paper offers an understanding of undocumented migrant women's position in Turkey and the role of the state in the light of migration, labour market regulations and sexual exploitation.

Gül İnce Beqo's paper, entitled *Family Perspective in Migration: A Qualitative Analysis on Turkish Families in Italy*, seeks to analyse, through a theoretical background and fieldwork, how ties with one's origins can affect the integration process of Turkish immigrants into Italian society and furthermore the impact of migration on family relations among recent Turkish immigrants in Italy. These aspects have been analysed in a qualitative study, where interviews were undertaken with first-generation Turkish migrants identified by snowballing sampling (N = 32 participants, two interviews for each family) who are currently residing in Novara, a city located in the Piedmont region in north-west Italy. Interview questions focused on history of the family, their migration choice, the comparison between 'here' and 'there', the migration experience and the changes on family relations, difficulties and community networks, etc. By considering an understudied community in Italy like the Turks, within a perspective of family relations, this study seeks to provide an original contribution to both the study of Turkish migration and family studies in general.

The research conducted on social capital focuses on both its advantages and disadvantages. The strict bonding feature of social capital to its members is one of these drawbacks. Thus the results of social capital in this concept trigger interpersonal oppression. Social capital might play a determining role in migration marriages. The networks which are effective in the occurrence of marriage involve social capital and can be transformed into tools of oppression. For that matter, gender roles might become significantly more evident and transformation in social gender might occur in the towns reached through immigration. Sevim Atila Demir and Pinar Yazgan, in their paper outline how marriages through social capital and social relationship networks of individuals living in Germany resulted in social capital issues and conflict. Secondly, they discuss the internal groups' views of increase in social control in marriages occurring through immigration. They also identify its effects on social gender and its transformation potential in parallel with the decrease in social control from the point of view of the external group. The in-depth interviews with eight divorced women are analysed within the frameworks of "social networks", "social capital", "oppression/confinement", "family pressure" and "consanguine relationships".

Pelin Sönmez's paper, entitled *Effects of the Refugee Crisis on Gender Policies: Studies on EU and Turkey,* presented EU and Turkish policies/initiatives for Syrian women citizens' integration with society. This was by employment and to make inferences on refugees' roles through the social reproduction process while their integration into the EU and Turkish societies is being observed. The main question in her paper is whether the EU may be a model Turkey, for the integration of refugee women into the labour market by using legal instruments and supportive policies. The answer(s) direct us to two specific questions for both Turkey and the EU. One is with regards how the 'domestic worker' phenomenon that has increased steadily since the 1950s would change in Turkey with the Syrian war and approximately 1.5 million women who are Syrian citizens living in Turkey. The second question in this research asks whether EU policies and initiatives for women could be a potential solution to the chronic aging population and decreasing employment problems within EU countries. Findings on these questions are correlated with A survey was carried out with 100 Syrian women citizens living in the Sultanbeyli district of Istanbul. It reflected on the employment capacity of Syrian citizen women living in Turkey and to consider possible future policies at the Turkish and EU levels.

References

Anthias, F. and Yuval-Davis, N. (1983). Contextualizing feminism: Gender, ethnic and class divisions. *Feminist Review*, 15: 62-75.

Blom, I. (1999). "Gender as an analytical tool in global history". In *Making Sense of Global History: The 19th International Congress of the historical Sciences*. Oslo, pp. 71-86. Accessed from https://www.oslo2000.uio.no/program/papers/m1a/M1a-blom.pdf, on 03 April 2017.

Bonney, N. and Love, J. (1991). Gender and migration: geographical mobility and the wife's sacrifice. *The Sociological Review*, 39 (2): 335-348.

Brettell, C. B. (2016). *Gender and Migration*. Cambridge: Polity Press.

Castles, S. and Miller, M. J. (2008). *Göçler Çağı*. İstanbul: İstanbul Bilgi Üniversitesi Yayınları.

Chant, S. (1992). "Conclusion: towards a framework for the analysis of gender-selective migration". In: *Gender and Migration in Developing Countries*, S. Chant (ed.). London: Belhaven Press, pp. 1-29.

Donato, K. M., Gabaccia, D., Holdaway, J., Manalansan, M., and Pessar, P. R. (2006). A glass half full? Gender in migration studies. *International migration review*, 40 (1): 3-26.

Fleury, A. (2016). *Understanding Women and Migration: A Literature Review*. KNOMAD Working Paper 8. Washington DC: The World Bank/Global Knowledge Partnership on Migration and Development (KNOMAD).

Gerson, K. (2004). Understanding work and family through a gender lens. *Community, Work and Family*, 7 (2): 163-178.

Giddens, A. and Sutton, P.W. (2014). *Sosyolojide Temel Kavramlar*. Translated by: A. Esgin. Ankara: Phoenix.

Jolly, S., Reeves, H. And Piper, N. (2005). *Gender and Migration: Overview Report*. Accessed from http://www.bdigital.unal.edu.co/39697/1/1858648661%20%282%29.pdf, on 21 January 2017.

Manalansan, M. F. (2006). Queer intersections: Sexuality and gender in migration studies. *International Migration Review*, 40 (1): 224-249.

Massey, D.S. (2015). A Missing Element in Migration Theories, *Migration Letters*, 12(3): 279-299.

Milewski, N., Sirkeci, I., Yüceşahin, M. M. and Rolls, A. (2015). *Family and Human Capital in Turkish Migration*. N. Milewski, I. Sirkeci, M.M. Yüceşahin and A. Rolls (eds.). London: Transnational Press London.

Piper, N. (2005). *Gender and Migration*. A paper prepared for the policy analysis and research programme of the global commission on international migration. Geneva: Global Commission on International Migration, 12. Accessed from https://www.iom.int/jahia/webdav/site/myjahiasite/shared/shared/mainsite/policy_and_research/gcim/tp/TP10.pdf, on 21 January 2017.

Ravenstein, E. G. (1885). The laws of migration. *Journal of the Statistical Society of London*, 48 (2): 167-235.

Shildrick, M. (1997). *Leaky Bodies and Boundaries: Feminism, Postmodernism and (Bio) Ethics*. London: Routledge.

Sirkeci, I. (2017). Turkey's refugees, Syrians and refugees from Turkey: a country of insecurity. *Migration Letters*, 14 (1): 127-144.

Sirkeci, I., Cohen, J. H. and Yazgan, P. (2012). Turkish culture of migration: Flows between Turkey and Germany, socio-economic development and conflict. *Migration Letters*, 9 (1): 33-46.

Slattery, M. (2015). *Sosyolojide Temel Fikirler*, Ü.Tatlıcan and G.Demiriz (eds.), (translated by Ö.Balkız, G. Demiriz, H. Harlak, C. Özdemir, Ş. Özkan, Ü. Tatlıcan). Bursa: Sentez Yayıncılık.

Sweetman, C. (1998). *Gender and Migration*. Oxford: Oxfam.

Thadani, V. N. and Todaro, M. P. (1984). "Female migration: A conceptual framework". In *Women in the Cities of Asia: Migration and Urban Adaptation*. J. T. Fawcett et al. (eds.), Boulder, CO: Westview Press, pp. 36-59.

Tilly, L. A. and Gurin, P. (1990). *Women, politics and change*. L. A. Tilly and P. Gurin (eds.). Newyork: Russell Sage Foundation.

Walby, S. (2007). *Gender in (Equality) and the Future of Work*. Manchester: Equal Opportunities Commission.

Walby, S. (1996). *Key Concepts in Feminist Theory*. Feminist Research Centre in Aalborg, Department of Development and Planning Aalborg University.

West, C. and Zimmerman, D. H. (1987). Doing gender. *Gender and Society*, 1 (2): 125-151.

Chapter Two

Deconstructing the Gender-Migration Relationship: Performativity and Representation

M. Murat Yüceşahin

Introduction

A rainbow variety of theories has been proposed to explain the underlying dynamics and reasons behind migration. The majority of the research in the field confirmed that the main motivation behind migration is the drive to attain a dignified standard of living with elevated economic, social, and environmental status. Not limited to economic developments alone, migration presents its obvious aspect, that it is "culturally produced, culturally expressed and cultural in effect" (Newbold, 2010: 136).

A close look at the nature of migration will immediately reveal its selective nature. "Migration selectivity"[1] manifests itself as the migration tendency that is determined only in accordance with various factors such as diverse characteristics of an individual's socio-demographic, socio-economic, and socio-cultural status (Yüceşahin *et al.*, 2015). Therefore it is obvious that this diversity in such characteristics as age, education, wealth, and other factors may or may not trigger migration, and at various levels of intensity, even if it does. Migration's highly selective nature further encourages us, the researchers, to take one step further into the depths, perhaps to review the gender aspect of this social phenomenon. A closer look at migrants' social and economic strategies and practices in transnational social spaces will walk us through some objective comparisons: While an overall

---

[1] Migration Selectivity, (also known as Differentiation) is the hypothesis presented by Todaro (1969) and Harris and Todaro (1970). It is basically the variability of migration based on various demographic characteristics such as age, sex, marital status, and also on income level and employment. Their seminal work based on a model of interregional migration is characterized by a certain degree of selectivity (Harris and Todaro, 1970).

comparison of men and women in terms of international migration reveals almost no difference in developed countries, the difference is much more distinct in less-developed countries where men show higher rates of migration in search of employment. Women, on the other hand, with much less mobility, and are identified as the care providers within the well-defined boundaries of households (Newbold, 2010: 138-139). Other comparisons on a scale of other socio-demographic indicators also play a role in migration selectivity. That is, factors such as marital status, parental status, and gender relations and practices significantly shape migration processes (Jolly and Reeves, 2005: 9), migrant selectivity, and the (re)production of transnational spaces.

Although there is no chronological timeline to pinpoint exactly when the gender-focused approach to migration first began, the first steps of this particular approach to migration studies were heard towards the end of the 19th century, thanks to well-known geographer E. G. Ravenstein (1885), who referred to the presence of some gender-perspective-related differences in migration patterns. The fact that these differences lacked in-depth analysis and were undocumented caused the gender approach to migration studies to remain obscure (Brettell, 2016: 1) until the 1970s, the years of feminist-based analyses first blooming with a focus shift on women's issues in social research. In line with the gradual growth of awareness and of the importance of studying migration-gender relations also in a multi-disciplinary perspective, feminist migration scholars shifted their focus from studying women towards studying "gender, as a system of relations which was influenced by migration" in the mid and late 1980s, (Richter, 2004: 263; Nawyn, 2010: 750). Since 1990, there has been an obvious increase in academic interest focusing on the "feminization of migration" (Bélanger and Linh, 2011: 60; Caritas Internationalis, 2012: 5), a concept corresponding with the dynamics of women's rising participation in international migration in recent years.

The post-modern era then unfolds its most important characteristics, which are the formation of a new stress field, a new pull-push polarity – between localization and increased globalism – and the self-manifestation of neoliberal policies in urban areas. The rise in the international mobility of populations in this new era triggered and is currently further increasing the interaction between the gender practices, norms, and cultural routines performed by such a variety of new identities in recently migrated areas. This is exactly why the significance of focusing on gender-migration relations in the context of post-modern dynamism is growing. It is through this dynamism that transnational social and all spaces are reconstructed or reproduced.

The relationship migration has with movement, or mobility[2]-gender[3], carries enough importance not to be downplayed solely to being addressed as gender inequality in migration/movement (Hanson, 2010). Studying the gender-migration relationship is certainly not easy either, due to the complexity inherent in its multifaceted nature and many other inputs inherent in this subject relationship.

The upsurge in globalization and technological developments not only facilitated the mobility of populations in the world but also created a new human capital, which led to the reconstruction of cosmopolitan geographies. Meanwhile, the boundaries and patterns of cities densely populated with international immigrants have been undergoing certain changes as triggered by the international mobility of populations. This trigger, along with how it is interwoven with the gender-migration fabric, causes cultural acts in the region of origin and total human capital to be transferred to the destination. What is actually transferred to the destination is far more than what is immediately visible: There are sets of experience and accumulated culture back in the immigrant's country of origin, such as the cumulative understanding of gender roles and gender practices; ways, perhaps routines, to cope with life challenges; what confirms and maintains the immigrant's identity, especially through gender roles and practices; and thus inequalities as possibly formed by and as reflection of their social strata, age, language, religion, ethnicity, education level, demographic features, etc. This is what turns transnational spaces into increasingly cosmopolitan, complex structures (Massey *et al.*, 1993: 431) from a migration-gender relation perspective. In fact, we cannot overstress at this point how not even the push-pull polarity of the economic activities between the country of origin and the destination is exempt from gender issues or from the migration-gender aspect being part of the pull-push polarity. Indeed, as Jarvis et al. stated: "The starting point of any gender analysis of migration has to be that economic push and pull factors are not gender neutral" (2009: 177).

---

[2] Contrary to the term "migration", the terms "movement" and "mobility" embody a somewhat more positive meaning as to refer to purposeful activities directed towards social spaces, freedom of movement, and free accessibility (Jarvis et al., 2009: 158).

[3] In social research the term gender is typically used to refer to social, psychological, and /or cultural differences between men and women, rather than biological sex differences (Knox and Pinch, 2010: 235).

As clearly seen, many receiving countries already present cultural textures in the neoliberal order to which the immigrant is generously welcomed to the existing gender inequality woven into the country's economy and market conditions. With some help from neo- and/or post-liberal influences, economies and market conditions of these countries are reconstructed as to neglect gender inequality. In fact, they reproduce the gender-based division of labour, segregation of private-public spaces, and inequalities (Molyneux, 2006; Cornwall *et al.*, 2008).

This is why it is crucial to ensure that gender-based approaches to migration take into account the inequality patterns both in sending and receiving countries (Brettell, 2016: 3). This is especially important as the dominant gender-regime from the sending countries – although with some possible variations from individual to household levels – is transferred to and therefore is likely to affect that of the receiving country, or vice-versa.

The dominant gender-regime of the receiving country, in response, may potentially grow hybrid with the influence from immigrants' gender practices in its diaspora/transnational spaces. This potential formation and process of a hybrid is then almost a result of the two colliding gender regimes (partly subject to be shaped by individual or household strategies and practices) and is therefore a focal interest of the gender analysis of migration. This is why migration is an inclusive process, and therefore deserves a comprehensive study, where complex relations in terms of gender practices and how they mutually interact and weave into one another are analysed.

Thus, the gender analysis of migration process addresses a set of complex relations of factors no longer limited to families, households, or women's lives, but expanded to a larger perspective as to include immigrants' lives and employment processes for both sexes, the politics and governance of migration, and neoliberal or welfare state policies toward migration or foreign-born populations in diasporas (Donato *et al.*, 2006: 6; Brettell, 2016: 6-7).

In this article, I aim to introduce a theoretical spatial approach to reach a resolution in gender-migration relation dynamics. While doing so, I bring together gender relations and practices of the country of origin and destination. My article centres on performativity and representation of migration-gender relations in terms of establishing transnational spaces. First I review gender practices of the migrating households in the scope of performative patriarchal power relations. In the second part, I then address the relations among gender, migration, and economic reconstruction in transnational spaces. Then in the last part I discuss the interactive transformation of gender and international migrational and urbanization processes within the scope of the reproduction of transnational social spaces.

Patriarchal Power in Migrant Households

A close look at historical aspects of gender relations will present us how the social structures and dynamics of early settlers led to the emergence of gender roles, roles typically resulting from the socio-psychological structures of early settling or from the division of labour between men and women, and in fact from the need to simply survive. In order to ensure survival, early humans had to adapt and live in decently formed groups as the earlier isolated smaller groups and their primitive methods and shelters left them highly vulnerable to hostile environments, challenging conditions, and ecological calamities. The most effective way to face the odds and survive would perhaps be best achieved if a silent social norm of division of labour were agreed upon, where perhaps men and women would shoulder responsibilities suited to their own abilities. While men undertook physical and ritual defence needs-related tasks such as being alert and ready to physically fight and perhaps take lives, women, biologically, were assigned "the role of life-giving, nurturing, preservation of the lives that were brought into being". A division of labour based on strengths further led women to improve their consequential attributes, namely the preservation of skills and knowledge of life-giving and bearing, and thus develop their femininity around the attributes of the settling of conflicts, caring, nurturing, gentleness, kindness, cooperation, accommodation of differences, perseverance, patience, acquiescence, and tolerance. Men, on the other hand, with their conquest and killer instinct, developed attributes such as decisiveness, ruthlessness, courage, confrontation, toughness, and intolerance of ambiguities.

In addition to this initial gap between the traits of men and women, another factor also added to women's submissive stance when women, with their responsibility for child-rearing from puberty to the grave, had a shorter life expectancy, an average lifespan of 30 years (Lerner, 1986; Miller, 2001). Unlike men, women thus missed the opportunity to join the elder members of the group, highly respected with their full representation of society's memory, and accumulated wisdom from experience facing all the trials of life. Unlike women, men, comparatively living longer[4], had the chance to further develop the role of being the entitled authority to hold the power to decide. Also with the life-taking end of the spectrum proving "more powerful than life-giving" in group dynamics in the long run, masculine traits' roots (Miller, 2001: 84-85) were gradually further enhanced and masculine roles gained a somewhat more assertive voice than that of women. That is, household dynamics were shaped where masculine power-holding father or men figures, initial exercisers of life-taking power and the ultimate voice of accumulated wisdom with a relatively longer lifespan, in time emerged as the final authority in all matters, including but not limited to the gender-based division of labour and power (Miller, 2001: 84-85). This consequence was certainly not foreseen when the early consensus on this division of labour, roles, and traits associated with responsibilities was reached. However, it is clear that the socio-psychosocial and cultural aspects of this division between men and women laid the foundations for the patriarchal structure and shaped the crucial role for today's mechanisms of gendered relations in societies, which in return shaped the dynamic definition of "gender".

In the trend of the gender definitions which began with the sexual division of labour and then evolved over time to another definition where the living space received its share of a highly gendered approach, thus drawing a restricted area for the household home sphere, it was liberalizing and extending the outer world for men (Dex, 1985; Reddock, 1994; Miller, 2001: 85). In line with the in-house roles of women in marriage as imposed by patriarchal ideology, women lacked any role in the decision-making process in outer-world related matters, and certainly not in any phase of the migration process.

A look at these gender-defined spaces – such as private-domestic spaces mostly for women, with public-urban spaces and expansive movement for men (Hanson, 2010: 9) – will also reflect on the contexts of mobility and migration and in fact on gender practices in the migration process. In all the stages of the migration process, there stands a masculine authority, which leads migration and mobility to be understood and represented in somewhat androcentric ways (Jarvis *et al.*, 2009: 158). For instance, decision-making and strategy-forming deeds regarding the prospective migration process fall within the jurisdiction of men. Women, with their

---

[4] "Conversely to the current gap between men and women in life expectancy, men lived longer than women, largely due to the risks attendant on child-bearing at that time" (Miller, 2001: 84).

rather diminished status in the decision-making process for the household's migration, indeed only highlighted their role and responsibility as the support and aid provider, and migration relocated and thus confirmed passive her stance.

In line with this particular range of assistant and/or aider roles expected from women and this particular blend of treatment and expectation towards women being built up in highly patriarchal household structures, the boundaries and degree of women's inclusion in the migration process were drawn. In other words, in patriarchal household dynamics, men, with their bestowed bread-winning role in the battlefield of the outer-world, held the hierarchical presumed and default role of decision-making in the entire spectrum of the migration process. The core patriarchal structure of the family in the country of origin led the migrating family to set up a copy-and-pasted parallelism to the country of destination. This aspect of the migration process, how migration hosts – within the actual process – the transfer of gender roles, or how migration and gender relations are interwoven during migration process, is concisely summarized by Brettell:

> "...there are two possible outcomes in terms of issues of gender and power that can characterize the migration process and the immigrant experience. If we take into account the relationship between the terms of gender and inequality, we can comprehend the power and prestige differences between men and women are gendered. Thus, sometimes for example, women face double discrimination not only as a migrant but also as a female because gender ideologies that are rooted in patriarchy may be transported if not sometimes even enhanced in the immigrant context. On the other hand, immigrant men, who may feel more disempowered in the public space or in jobs in which they have clearly experienced downward mobility, may try to exercise more control their wives and children in the private space" (2016: 4).

In many migration cases of blue-collar workers from Turkey to European countries such as Germany, France, Belgium, Sweden, etc., an expected pattern almost most certainly applies: It is only after men attain a certain level of material success in corporate life and a regular salary in the country of destination that the other household members would then migrate to the solidified castle of house or life built, meaning the castle of social success built by men. The scope of responsibility both in the process and post phases of migration, in women's case, would be to ensure complete care for the well-being of the in-house needs of their children, and probably those of the elderly, normally the men's parents. A slight shift and weakening in the patriarchal set of gender relations might be observed upon facing various challenges and shifts in lifestyles such as women's employment and financial contribution to the household. However, even in the case of such a possible seeming reallocation in the overall patriarchal roof of the house, all these would develop on the basis of a consensus, that is the patriarchal household decisions on the distinction of private and corporate spaces. That is, even at the migrated destination, all these are confirmed and reassured in line with some sort of patriarchal agreement reached among the household members. Under this agreement, men are bestowed once again the earlier-confirmed roles and are ensured to hold the sole authority both in the private and corporate spaces in the migrated country. Women, on the other hand, once again are designated in line with the previous consensus of cultural norms and values, which means providing care (as "loyalty") to all the household members (Naldemirci, 2015) within the boundaries of home, somewhat isolated from the outer world.

Gender-Based Economic (Re)structuring in Receiving Countries

In line with industrial production, the definition of space has become more distinct, such as Home versus Work. Women have always made economic contributions whether at home or anywhere else, but it was not until the 19th century that women started working for businesses in exchange for salaries, and therefore started challenging the notion that their only proper place was their very own home. This formed the basis for their argument to further gain the right to employment (McDowell, 2007: 123). However, they were only able to secure themselves the jobs and spaces in the business world seen as apt and "tailored" to fit women. As of the mid-20th century, women's paid employment increased rapidly, with an increase in specific work types, or rather jobs seen as "women appropriate". This gender-specific segregation is widespread even in today's work landscape. Therefore the key issue for feminist sociologists, economists, and economic geographers has been to explain the reasons for women's initial exclusion and then their concentration in specific work types and places and segregation within the labour market (McDowell, 2007: 123-124; Yüceşahin, 2016: 92-93).

Neglected in the economic structures of the many countries, gender inequality shows itself quite distinctly in labour market conditions, especially towards immigrants (Fleury, 2016: 9). That is, an immigrant would first face challenges of filtering structures formed both by components of local culture and by gender-based hierarchies in the destination country, then overcome these challenges to secure employment. This was verified by Broughton (2008: 569) and Jarvis et al. (2009: 179-180) when they presented actual cases and explanations regarding Mexican immigrants in the U.S. When its economy is need of a workforce, the receiving country preserves and maintains its continual gendered labour market and practices to which international immigrants are welcomed[5].

When gender differences are scrutinized through the lens of geographical analyses of migration, we can gradually view how power is placed spatially and also witness "insight into the gender dimensions of the social construction of scale, the socio-spatial (re)production in relation to gender roles and practices" (Silvey, 2006: 64). In today's world, there still exist highly distinct geographical variations when it comes to employment and women's participation in the workforce (McDowell, 2007: 125).

In almost every country, this stems from economic reproduction being based on the private-public distinction and from the fact that women are denied public jobs. That is, women are perceived as "clients and receivers, rather than providers of welfare" within the reproduction of labour in many globalizing countries (Kofman and Raghuram, 2006: 283). We could substantiate the case by providing concrete examples from many regions or countries worldwide, all showing how migration processes and gendered labour market conditions interact. At this point I will continue my argument based on an extreme case. There exists an explicit migration-gender inequality in the labour markets of receiver countries, especially those with the petroleum-based industry and with an economy fuelled by capital-intensive production.

For instance, parallel to the rise of petroleum-based economies in the Middle East, in 1955-1975 this caused the relevant Gulf countries (Kuwait, Oman, Qatar, Saudi Arabia, Bahrain, and the United Arab Emirates) along with Iraq and Libya, to suffer from labour shortages, contrary to their capital wealth. An intensive flow of a male labour force started mostly from Egypt, Jordan, the West Bank, Tunisia, Yemen, and Lebanon into these mentioned countries, which in return led to a striking flow of foreign currency – through the employed labourers – into the sender countries' economies. These oil-rich countries started to become attractive for other countries with large labour forces such as South Korea, the Philippines,

---

[5] Men and women in sending countries may be differently affected by policies, resulting in gendered patterns of migration; laws regarding both emigration and immigration are often strongly gendered; and policies that affect the integration of migrants into receiving societies may also affect men and women differently (Piper, 2006: 133-134).

and Sri Lanka. For instance, Gulf countries had a foreign labour force of 47% in 1975, rising dramatically to 68% in 1990. That same year some 86% of Kuwait's workforce was comprised of foreign workers (Moghadam and Decker, 2013: 76-77).

Modernization and state and economic restructuring in the MENA (Middle East and North Africa) region in the 1950s-1970s triggered a change process in social structures and provided new jobs and field of expertise for the contemporary middle class and labourers. That new types of jobs were created in the industry and service sectors and their introduction to the market somehow initiated women's employment.

For instance, when women in Turkey and in Egypt secured themselves more and more employment making economic contributions to commercial and industrial enterprises in public sectors, the domino effect this had on the region was similar, with the novelty of women being employed as teachers and healthcare personnel in higher numbers. Governments in the MENA region also embarked on an innovation during their economic growth and addressed the needs of working mothers. They not only institutionalized social insurance programs but also solidified protections of their legal rights, ensuring the inclusion of paid maternal leave and childcare fringe benefits.

However, the majority of the population was not employed in the public sector, but instead, in agricultural production and traditional commerce. The concentration of employment in these sectors led the social welfare regime of the MENA region to be built on family, as the key institution, during the oil wealth era. As long as oil revenues remained high and the economy grew, the informal family production and foreign currency input by labourers continued playing a great role in solidifying socio-economic well-being, at least for a certain part of the society. However, this structure failed to be part of society's official welfare system. Whether in the formal or informal sector, men were the breadwinners. Up until the new century, this was the answer to why women's participation in non-agricultural sectors remained so low. The actual answer was hidden to a large extent in the region's political economy: Petrol-based growth and capital-intensive production were both gendered and highly restrictive in women's allowed labour roles and demand. Those at the centre and blessed with the relatively higher salaries of the oil sector were male labourers. During the rise of the petrol sector, the structure was built to have male labourers as the recipients of the highest salaries, and therefore to have recruitment of women at a minimal level and with lowest salaries possible. This narrowed down recruitment possibilities for women in search of jobs.

This patriarchal structure established on a gender-relations consensus defined men as breadwinning actors, while defining the social identity of their spouses, children, and elderly parents as parties in need of men's financial support (The World Bank, 2004: 20; Moghadam and Decker, 2013: 78). Defined as spouse, mother, housewife, and care provider, women's social roles were confirmed also in this direction not only in the highly patriarchal society but also in the family law of the region as well. That is, both the political economy and family law contributed to processes restricting women's participation in the economy, and to gender-based segregation of private-public spaces (Moghadam and Decker, 2013: 78; Fenster and Hamdan-Saliba, 2013: 535).

In the mid-1980s, due to the slowdown of the petrol-based economic era and its eventual halt with labourers' return to their home countries, the resulting economic blow caused a significant decrease in household income and an increase in unemployment. This certainly affected men, but the most adverse effect was seen when it grew even harder for women and the young to secure employment. Despite the upsurge in the number of women seeking employment, the unemployment rate for women increased rapidly in the 1990s, which is the true indicator of need for labour force (Moghadam & Decker, 2013: 79). All these trends and gendered social, economic, and political transformations in the region led to male-dominated transnational migration towards countries with oil-enriched economies and then to an extremely asymmetrical distributions of the population by age and sex in Gulf States. Oman is a perfect example as shown in Figure 2.1, which shows the distribution of the country's population by age group and sex in 1960, 1990, and 2015.

As clearly seen in this figure, there is an obvious pileup formed due to male workers' migration increase – especially for those in the employable age range – and male dominance of the population in a 55-year period following the 1960s, especially in 1990 and 2015. The distinct asymmetry in the distribution of population by employed men and women is a clear reflection of the gender inequality presence in the economic structure.

In fact the population pyramids similar to the figures can be seen almost in all Gulf countries' social structures, where sex-ratio gaps are higher than any other societies in the world. For instance, in 2010-15, the sex ratio[6] of

---

[6] Sex ratio is the ratio of the number of males to the number of females, usually expressed as males per 100 females. The natural sex ratio at birth is typically around 105 males per 100 females. Small departures from this level may reflect random variations, while large departures forewarn of rarely possible data quality issues but in general, social and migration influences.

the total population in Saudi Arabia was 130.1 and 128.2 in Kuwait (140.7 in the term 1990-95). This ratio was 197 in Oman, 265.5 in Qatar, 163 in Bahrain, and 274 in the United Arab Emirates (UN, 2016a). In these and other labourer immigrant receiver countries, the gender comparison ratio by age is indeed high, especially within the employment age range of 20-39. We certainly cannot expect all receiver countries to have such a high gender ratio in their total population due to immigration. However, as Jarvis et al. (2009: 177) state, the fact that many jobs and work types have been gender-divided already highlights the gendered economy structure of the receiver country.

Figure 2.1. Distribution of population by age group and sex in Oman in 1960, 1990, and 2015

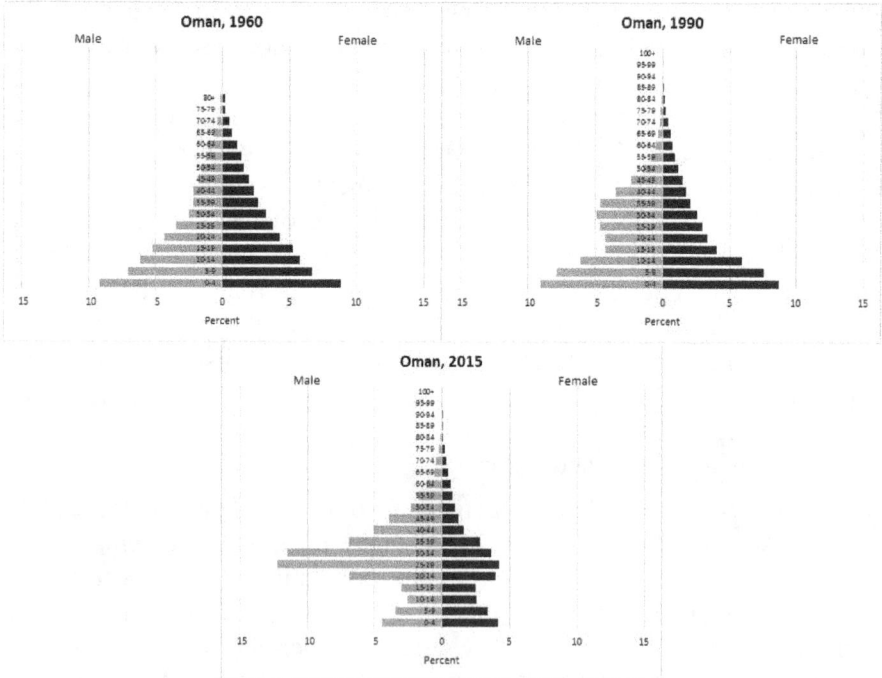

Data Source: UN (2016a); author's calculations.

Gender, International Migration, and Urbanization in Transnational Social Spaces

More specifically, migration influences sex ratios (of total populations), particularly at younger working ages where there may be an over-representation of male migrants (Rowland, 2006: 87-88).

The interactive transformation of gender, international migration, and urbanization processes in recent years suggests significant trends and thus some projections for the future. The first of these projections is that the world's urban population could reach up to 70% by 2050. In line with the projection that urbanization will continue to rise in all countries regardless of their level of development (Figure 2.2), it is obvious that the trend to live in urban areas has reached a level that has long been irreversible (Jarvis et al., 2009: 181).

Second, another trend emerges which is a set of factors interacting with one another – such as neo-liberalization and globalization leading to migration and migration to diasporas – and which thus is contributing to the urbanization process. Therefore the relationship built by international migration and diasporas to link with urbanization and gender issues gains prominence and visibility. The interacting dynamics of gender and the urbanization process should be approached from the neoliberalization and globalization perspective (Jarvis et al., 2009: 181). The fact that the term "urbanization of neoliberalism" is increasingly referred to in the literature clearly shows that neoliberalism produces itself based on and in relation to urban spaces. Today urban spaces stand out as the most important centres where neoliberalism reproduces itself with its political-ideological tools, corporate novelties and projects, and where it undergoes mutation (Brenner & Theodore, 2002: 375).

Neoliberalism, due to its heterosexist and hegemonic approach, spreads a certain ideology which neglects, legitimizes, and further enhances gender inequality in urban politics and daily life (Brenner and Theodore, 2002; Cornwall, et al., 2008; Jarvis et al., 2009). The way neoliberalism and the capitalist order neglects gender inequality also leaves metropolitan cities of the international migrant receiver countries defenceless against these trends. Once these trends are fully absorbed, the inequality issues continue, remaining unresolved.

Third, the percentage of women immigrants soared significantly at the global scale towards the new millennium (Kofman and Raghuram, 2006: 282; Jarvis et al., 2009: 181). This was the result of workforce-related dynamics. Economy-trend determiners rendered underdeveloped countries' labour forces open to the effect of globalization processes, eventually comprising the labour force more and more of women, increasing the number of fragmented families, with the male figures being urged to secure employment abroad. Another contributing factor is unfortunately linked with the increase in sex trafficking of women and children due to the demand by multinational companies contracting with low-cost labour provider countries such as China and Taiwan. (Jarvis et al., 2009: 182). As seen in Figure 2.1, depending on how different cultures define the employment of men and women, migration flows play a significant role in the gender structure and urban areas or countries' sex ratio of the total populations.

Figure 2.2. Annual percentage of population at mid-year residing in urban areas by region and the world overall, 1950-2050

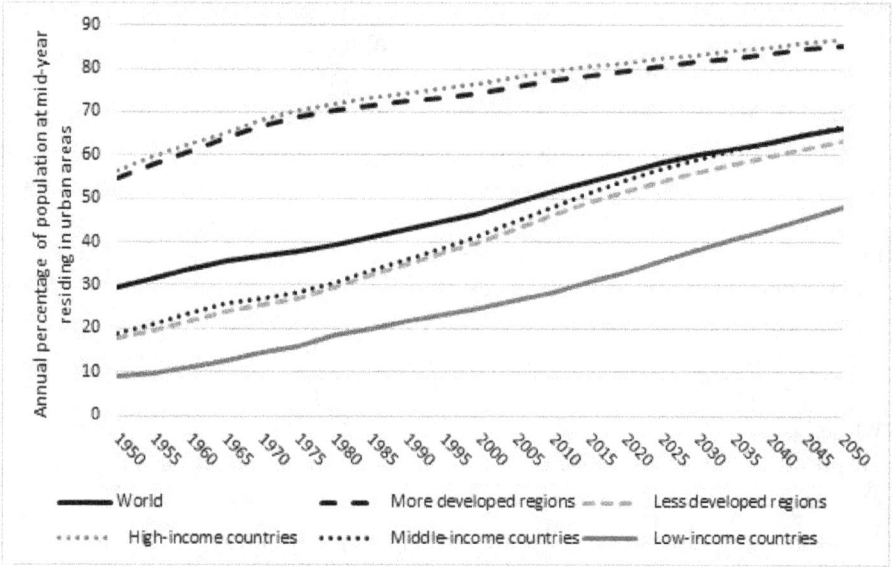

Data source: UN (2016b).

For a last point, as a result of finance-motivated transnational migrations, new household and family functions emerge where women may provide cross-border financial care. These families, characterized by their cross-border functions, enrich the family formations in the destination countries while women in local spaces remain in their care-provider roles (Jarvis et al., 2009: 182).

The interaction and thus restructuring of cities and transnational spaces in terms of globalization, neoliberalism, and gender relations is worth studying as well. Throughout history and across cultures, spatial arrangements and architectural constructions have always been a dimension in gender relations; they are spatial representations of the details of patriarchy, full of references to reinforce status differences between women and men (Spain, 2005: 43). As pointed out by Doreen Massey and Daphne Spain, there is a direct bilateral interaction between how space is socially and how the social structure of relationships is constructed based on space features (Massey, 1994: 22; Spain, 2005: 44). Thus, cities with their spatial features indeed create, define, and act as a mirror for gender roles and practices. They also reflect and reproduce systems of patriarchy and are hetero-patriarchal environments[7]. Thus, it is important to recognize the diversity of the city at this point; the categories "man" and "woman" are cut across by divisions of class, age, ethnicity, immigration, religion, etc. (Knox and Pinch, 2010: 236).

The gendered structure of cities is visible where men are granted the privilege of having access to knowledge to produce and reproduce power within daily life. Within the aggressive, male-dominated business environment, especially in public but also in private domestic spheres, women are only granted the access to a certain level in the career paths, provided that they not only perform well at their jobs, but also can manoeuvre gracefully through sexist comments reminding them of their "otherness". Interestingly, the city is also an environment characterized by heterosexual values and norms and homophobia (Knox and Pinch, 2010: 237).

One of the most basic features of transnational spaces resulting from international migration is that they are where socio-demographic features – such as class, age, migration status, religion – and the gender relations of a society intersect and blend to form the result of a new structure. The most striking geographical restructuring in urban social spaces is built by various layers of diverse minorities or immigrant groups, especially through their clustering and/or segregation process. Granted, there are theoretical explanations which address the dynamics behind spatial clustering and/or segregation processes in urban societies densely populated with international immigrants. However the process is initiated when the group identity is formed, as a first step – that is, when the local population starts determining and identifying "the others" or what constitutes "the others". This identification process is carried out by means of discriminative-static perceptions and stereotypes and by representative wordings of "us" versus "them" (Knox and Marston, 2014: 414; Van Dijk et al., 2015: 91).

---

[7] The broad system of social arrangements and institutional structures that enable men to dominate women is generally known as "patriarchy". Since patriarchy is dominated by heterosexual values, this is also termed "heteropatriarchy". Consequently, areas of cities dominated by these values are often termed "heteropatriarchal environments" (Knox and Pinch, 2010: 235-236).

Reservations, concerns, and fears regarding contacts with "the other", which cluster group members with their representative identities but only segregates them from others, also brings with themselves individual and institutionalized discriminations in terms of characteristics such as class, culture, gender, ethnicity, and race (Nightingale, 2012: 4; Knox and Marston, 2014: 414; French, 2014: 389).

The clustering of diverse immigrant groups in urban spaces is an expression, although not always voluntary, which stems from the need to establish and preserve group identity and lifestyles, and this expression draws strength from the immigrants' relevant practices and rituals (Knox and Pinch, 2010: 165; Knox and Marston, 2014: 414).

The fact that the social groups, immigrants, aim to settle down in different spatial areas initiates processes such as becoming coherent with the space-settled isolation from "the other". The first one, growing coherent with the space, mostly depends on membership scales (origin, migration movements in the past and present, religion, language, physical appearance); personal goals (interests, solidarity in a foreign land, etc.); all rules and norms including practices (e.g. gender roles); and on group relations and the allocation of resources (Van Dijk et al., 2015: 43). The second, being somewhat isolated, is expected: Settling down in different spatial areas also facilitates the restriction of social interaction with what is defined as "the other". That is why immigrant groups interact and conduct their life practices, including their marriages, with those from their own social groups and/or those with more or less equal social statuses and similar cultural and identity textures.

Therefore, gender norms of the local culture find a way to somehow protect themselves and actually continue to exist, after being transferred to the deep-rooted structure of the transnational spaces. Certainly there is a correlation between the interaction level with the local population of the receiver country and thus the integration degree which would eventually lead to some blending and modifications in the immigrants' gender practices. However, since patriarchal power and its representation is quite widespread in the world, neither a full and healthy interaction with the transnational space nor a fully healthy process of change in the set of gender regimes transferred from the country of origin seems likely. Rather, the gender regime transferred to the receiver country plants its own seeds and flourishes through restructuring itself with the gendered policies particular to the immigrants of transnational spaces (Brettell, 2016: 8-9). At this point, the neoliberal policies and gendered labour markets do not seem to help either, as it is exactly these components of urban spaces which disadvantage women in comparison to any but especially immigrant men's likelihood of employment.

Gender inequality transferred by immigrants secures itself against possible change through a very basic instinct: The group's will to protect its identity and cultural values usually manifests itself through the protection of the archaic gender roles, and the gendered division of labour especially under poor financial conditions, where men are the party to shoulder financial responsibility. During these difficult times, the high stress suffered also finds its way to reach women immigrants first, with men likely to resort to domestic violence against women, leaving them all the more vulnerable and fragile (Jarvis et al., 2009: 180). Prior and post-migration processes somehow render mostly women, rather than men, to be gender-discriminated due to factors such as neoliberalism, globalization, and transnationalism.

Conclusion

Although sharing common default structures in almost all societies, gender regimes also show variations, due to such spectrums of inequalities particular to the subject local spaces. Especially international migration initially not only transfers the local-specific gender-based hierarchical structures to other locations of the world, but also brings together and most importantly transforms the brand-new pieces of various forms of hierarchies into the settled country. Therefore this brings to the surface the opposites and polarizations in terms of gender relations and new identity acts especially in cities embodying transnational societies.

As a result of contacts with other social circles through migration experience, some multifaceted processes emerge, encompassing within themselves households' transformations and/or default definitions growing inflexible. As McDowell also stresses, migration may in fact be an experience where loyalty towards all the notions and norms carried from the country of origin may even grow stronger:

> *"Migration may lead to a clinging to old notions of identity and a desire to reject the new experiences as often as to a progressive transformation of identity through the breaking down of old binary distinctions" (2007: 220).*

As the above clearly shows, migration brings together cultural performances of the country of origin and of destination, in transnational spaces. Even if transformations in these spaces hold the ability to reshape gender roles and norms, these transformations may be somehow invisible, with the local-specific components being complicated and part of a melting pot of a metropolitan structure. Migration needs to be understood as a social, economic, and political process upon which immigrants' life and gender practices are reflected as indispensable components (Silvey, 2004: 495; Jarvis et al., 2009: 181).

It is certainly important to underline the macro-level role played by transnational political and economic conditions, globalization, and neoliberal processes. This way or the other, migration movement occurs within the triangle formed by the local-specific patriarchal power hierarchies, the gender mechanism of global labour forces, and the reproduction of transnational social spaces; it forms an intersectional field. Power-based hierarchy within the patriarchal texture of culture organizes social and economic policies and spaces at all stages of migration starting from the early stages of decision-making to migrate or not, then migration itself, and later the resettlement processes.

Once we address inequality in gender imbalances (Brettell, 2016: 4), we have to recognize that migration folds inequality into two, from women's perspective. In fact, women are not the only party to be disadvantaged in gender inequality strategies. Those who stand high up, in terms of their recognized source of power, in the hierarchy of hetero-patriarchal structure – for instance LGBT individuals or others – somehow turn into the sole owners of the lower statuses in the entirety of society. That is migration itself, and being an immigrant or woman, or occupying a lower status on any hierarchy will mean exposure to various forms of inequality for individuals or groups.

In comparison to other forms of mobility, migration and being an immigrant is full of more negative attributes and meanings. Immigrant women or social groups therefore shoulder a double inequality burden and end up encountering discrimination at much higher levels.

Being an immigrant is interwoven with gendered transnational spaces, unequal spatial structures formed based on race, social stratum, ethnicity, and education level. This blend eventually places immigrants on a re-production platform where they are bound to suffer even further disadvantages. As per the immigrants' reaction to that negative structuring, this reaction first starts by forming some kind of resistance mechanism against the unknown conditions and taking measures against the fear of losing cultural values. The first and most important mechanism to preserve what is defined as the identity against the new environment is to ensure that gender roles and practices are maintained and nurtured, and to develop strategies to strictly protect the "good old" however known, safe and home-defined practices. The final structure formed based on this conservative approach then brings about an introverted culture focusing on its truly and desperately owned cultural values by the immigrants/minority group. Patriarchal structure's need to assure itself as the strong role – as opposed to the discriminated and culturally suppressed role by the new settlement conditions – finds a highly secure source to quench its thirst: The family unit where the formerly and culturally recognized patriarchal role is to be preserved through the power exercised on another "other", this time the already suppressed party, women. Imposing gendered roles not only helps the socially unwelcomed patriarchal party reclaim their glory and be redefined through women's secondary role, but also allows the defeated "hunter', "gatherer', "fighter" of the outer world to turn into a power-holder, only where women are defined as means only to serve their "raison d'être" confirmation of a male proficiency self-assurance and self-confirmation. This focus by the power-holder will then conduct its self-assurance of "d'être" by means of certain available components such as immigrants' ethnicity, identity, "honour", and religious values, all of which are easiest to raise on the party ready to submit and adapt already: Immigrant women who have been gender-discriminated during the migration process under the excuse of being assigned the "proper" centuries-long roles in the survival-focused mode of the family unit, a mode which produces and reinforces survival-justified, and therefore much stricter, intolerable fabrics of rules. The final structure all these eventually bring about is a higher conservatism displayed and justified by the immigrant/minority group, especially when the group dynamics grow even more introvert and closed around the axis of what they claim as protecting their cultural identities, values, or "family honour" as claimed. Since this highly justified protection of family honour finds its easiest way through exerting power on lower-status holders, namely women or the like, this new immigrant group dynamics increases the probability of transforming women into a social group that is prone to being vulnerable to all risks in transnational spaces.

Values and social norms of the origin country which are transferred to the receiver country will certainly be open to some effect imposed by how the existing integration and gender policies of the settled country are exercised. Gender practices by the immigrants may be positively affected only through the social policies and practices based on equality principles. However, it is observed that metropolitan cities as the receiver of the largest number of immigrants are not immune from structures shaped by neoliberal and globalization, where a gender-discriminative division of labour makes equality for immigrant women mostly neglected.

Therefore, while studying migration from a wide, bird's-eye view perspective, we are greeted by the complexity of three main spatial components of the migration process in close interaction with one another, namely: first, immigrant household's patriarchal power relations existing in their space of origin; second, the transfer process of all set of patriarchal relations to the psycho-social and economic structure of the settlement space set to receive; and, third and last, transnational space as the component where the received set of gender relations are blended to perhaps form an integrated set of patriarchal structures. Within the interaction of all these three dynamics stands an immigrant whose new identity is also in the process of being re-established in the transnational space in light of their socio-demographic-attributed roles and gender-defined "culturally assigned roles" and practices – all of which contribute to their segregation. Exposed to the pressure resulting from the interaction of all these, the international immigrant is then urged to develop survival skills and to form survival clusters in certain spaces where their gender roles and practices are prominent and are explicitly performed and represented in addition to their cultural components such as language, religion, education level, and occupation.

References

Bélanger, D. and Linh, T. G. (2011). The impact of transnational migration on gender and marriage in sending communities of Vietnam. *Current Sociology*, 59 (1): 59-77.

Brenner, N. and Theodore, N. (2002). Cities and the geographies of 'actually existing neoliberalism. *Antipode*, 34 (3): 349-379.

Brettell, C. B. (2016). *Gender and Migration*. Cambridge: Polity Press.

Broughton, C. (2008). Migration as engendered practice: Mexican men, masculinity, and Northward migration. *Gender and Society*, 22 (5): 568-589.

Caritas Internationalis. (2012). *The Female Face of Migration: Advocacy and Best Practices for Women Who Migrate and the Families They Have Leave Behind*. Caritas International Working Document. 17 February 2012. Vatican: Ems Creative. https://www.caritas.org/includes/pdf/advocacy/ FFMCaritas Policy Doc.pdf, Accessed on 8 January 2017.

Cornwall, A., Gideon, J. and Wilson, K. (2008). Introduction: Reclaiming feminism: Gender and neoliberalism. *IDS Bulletin*, 39 (6).

Dex, S. (1985). The Sexual Division of Work: Conceptual Revolutions in the Social Sciences. Brighton: Wheatsheaf Books Harvester Press.

Donato, K. M., Gabaccia, D., Holdaway, J., Manalansan IV, M. and Pessar, P. R. (2006). A glass half full? Gender in migration studies. *International Migration Review*, 40 (1): 3-26.

Fenster, T. and Hamdan-Saliba, H. (2013). Gender and feminist geographies in the Middle East. *Gender, Place and Culture: A Journal of Feminist Geography*, 20 (4): 528-546.

Fleury, A. (2016). *Understanding Women and Migration: A Literature Review*. Global Knowledge Partnership on Migration and Development (KNOMAD) Working Paper 8. Accessed from http://www.knomad.org/docs/gender/KNOMAD %20Working%20Paper%208%20final_Formatted.pdf, on 12 January 2017.

French, K. N. (2014). "Exploring Socioeconomic Characteristics of Ethnically Divided Neighbourhoods". In *Social-Spatial Segregation: Concepts, Processes and Outcomes,* C. D. Lloyd, I. G. Shuttleworth and D. W. S. Wong (eds.), Bristol: Policy Press, pp. 389-412.

Hanson, S. (2010). Gender and mobility: new approaches for informing sustainability. *Gender, Place and Culture: A Journal of Feminist Geography*, 17 (1): 5-23.

Harris, J. R. and Todaro, M. P. (1970). Migration, unemployment, and development: A two-sector analysis. *American Economic Review* 61: 26-141.

Jarvis, H., Kantor, P. and Cloke, J. (2009). *Cities and Gender*. London: Routledge, Taylor & Francis Group.

Jolly, S. and Reeves, H. (2005). *Gender and Migration*. Overview Report. BRIDGE Institute of Development Studies. http://www.bridge.ids.ac.uk/ sites/ bridge. ids. ac.uk/files/reports/CEP-Mig-OR.pdf, Accessed on 10 January 2017.

Knox, P. L. and Marston, S. A., (2014). *Human Geography: Places and Regions in Global Context*. Essex: Pearson.

Knox, P. and Pinch, S. (2010). *Urban Social Geography: An Introduction.* Sixth edition, London: Prentice Hall.

Kofman, E. and Raghuram, P. (2006). Gender and global labour migrations: Incorporating skilled workers. *Antipode*, 38 (2): 282-303.

Massey, D. (1994). *Space, Place, and Gender*. Minneapolis: University of Minnesota Press.

Massey, D. S., Arango, J., Hugo, G., Kouaouci, A., Pellegrino, A. and Taylor, J. E. (1993). Theories of international migration: A review and appraisal. *Population and Development Review*, 19 (3): 431-466.

McDowell, L. (2007). *Gender, Identity and Space: Understanding Feminist Geographies*. Third edition. Minneapolis: University of Minnesota Press.

Milewski, N., Sirkeci, I., Yüceşahin, M.M. and Rolls, A.S. (eds.). (2015). *Family and Human Capital in Turkish Migration*. London: Transnational Press London.

Miller, E. (2001). "Gender, power and politics: An alternative perspective". In *Gender, Peace and Conflict*, I. Skjelsbaek and D. Smith (eds.), London: Sage Publications, pp. 80-103.

Moghadam, V. M. and Decker, T. (2013). "Social change in the Middle East". In *The Middle East*, E. Lust (ed.). London: CQ Press, pp. 73-106.

Molyneux M. (2006). Mothers at the service of the new poverty agenda: Progresa / Oportunidades, Mexico's Conditional Transfer Programme. *School Policy and Administration*, 40 (4): 425-449.

Naldemirci, Ö. (2015). "Rethinking loyalty (vefa) through transnational care practices of older Turkish women in Sweden". In: N. Milewski, I. Sirkeci, M. M. Yüceşahin, and A. S. Rolls (eds.). *Family and Human Capital in Turkish Migration*. London: Transnational Press London, pp. 35-45.

Nawyn, S. J. (2010). Gender and migration: Integrating feminist theory into migration studies. *Sociology Compass*, 4 (9): 749-765.

Newbold, K. B. (2010). *Population Geography: Tools and Issues*. Rowman & Littlefield Publishers, Inc., Lanham.

Nightingale, C. H. (2012). *Segregation: A Global History of Divided Cities*. Chicago: The University of Chicago Press.

Piper, N. (2006). Gendering the politics of migration. *International Migration Review*, 40 (1): 133-164.

Ravenstein, E. G. (1885). The laws of migration. *Journal of the Statistical Society of London* 48: 167-235.

Reddock, R. E. (1994). *Women, Labour & Politics in Trinidad &Tobago: A History*. Kingston: Ian Randle Publishers.

Richter, M. (2004). Contextualizing gender and migration: Galician immigration to Switzerland. *International Migration Review*, 38 (1): 263-286.

Rowland, D. T. (2012). *Demographic Methods and Concepts*. New York: Oxford University Press.

Silvey, R. (2006). Geographies of gender and migration: Spatializing social difference. *International Migration Review*, 40 (1): 64-81.

Silvey, R. (2004). Power, difference and mobility: feminist advances in migration studies. *Progress in Human Geography*, 28 (4): 490-506.

Spain D. (2005). "Space and status". In: N. Kleniewski (ed.). *Cities and Society*. Malden: Blackwell Publishing, pp. 43-53.

The World Bank. (2004). Mena Development Report, Gender and Development in the Middle East and North Africa: Women in the Public Sphere. Washington, D.C.: The World Bank.

Todaro, M. P. (1969). A model of labour migration and urban unemployment in less developed countries. *American Economic Review*, 60: 138-148.

UN (United Nations) (2016a). *World Population Prospects, the 2015 Revision Data Base*. Department of Economic and Social Affairs. Accessed from https://esa.un.org/unpd/wpp/DataQuery/, on 7 November 2016.

UN (United Nations) (2016b). *World Urbanization Prospects, the 2014 Revision Data Base*. Department of Economic and Social Affairs. https://esa.un.org/unpd/wup/DataQuery/, Accessed on 15 December 2016.

Van Dijk, T., Wilson, J., Fairclough, N., Graham, P., Çoban, B., Ataman, B., Springer, S., Nail, T. and Köse, D. (2015). *Söylem ve İdeoloji [Discourse and Ideology]*. İstanbul: Su Press.

Yüceşahin, M. M. (2016). Toplumsal cinsiyet ve mekânın karşılıklı ilişkisi: Patriyarkanın sosyal mekânı örgütleyişine dair bir tartışma [Gender and space in reciprocal relation: A discussion on the structuring of social space by patriarchy]. *Kadın / Woman 2000: Kadın Araştırmaları Dergisi / Journal for Women's Studies*, 17 (1): 73-101.

Yüceşahin, M. M., Milewski, N., Sirkeci, I. and Rolls, A. S. (2015). "Introduction: Family and demography in Turkish mobility". In: N. Milewski, I. Sirkeci, M. M. Yüceşahin, and A. S. Rolls (eds.). *Family and Human Capital in Turkish Migration*. London: Transnational Press London, pp. 1-10.

Chapter Three

Gendered Pathways: Central Asian Migration through the Lens of Embodiment

Natalia Zotova and **Victor Agadjanian**

Introduction

The collapse of the Soviet Union in 1991 gave a start to mass international migration (Heleniak, 2008). Migration flows were first fueled by the regional insurgence, ethnic conflicts and civil war in Tajikistan (1992-1997), subsequent instability and economic turmoil. The shift from limited spatial mobility to development of massive population flows happened in a short historic span. While Russia became the destination country of choice for labor migrants from former Soviet states (Heleniak, 2008; Abashin, 2014), the patterns of mobility, motives and participants changed over time. Migration from Central Asian countries is fueled by economic difficulties; however, the causes of migration should not be limited to economic terms only. Rather they could be defined in a broader context of human insecurity.

Central Asian migration is dynamic. Russia still remains the destination of choice for the majority of Central Asian migrants. Although Moscow, the Russian capital and by far the largest city, has been a primary magnet for these migrants, the destinations of migration flows have been diversifying to include other big Russian cities. Overall, in 2016 Russia's Ministry of Internal Affairs has reported almost 5 million entries of Central Asian natives to the country. Women have come to constitute an increasingly large share of the migration flow; and account from 13% for Tajikistan and Uzbekistan natives to almost 40% for Kyrgyzstan migrants (MIARF, 2016). Most of migrants, men and women alike, have irregular legal status (e.g., lacking migration registration, residential registration, or work permit) and therefore are often marginalized, harassed, and exploited by their employers and law enforcing officials. Central Asian migrants' ethnoracial background (darker skin, limited Russian language proficiency) and religion add to their economic and legal marginalization (Agadjanian and Zotova, 2014). Exclusion of migrants allows them for a limited choice of occupation, and they settle for low skilled service positions, construction or other manual jobs (Zotova and Cohen, 2016).

Geographic position, visa waiver bilateral agreements and developed social networks continue to attract the majority of Central Asian migrants to Russia. However, in response to accumulated knowledge of xenophobia and anti-Muslim sentiments in Russia, economic trouble and new laws limiting entry and employment opportunities, Central Asian movers start looking for new destinations which include European countries, Turkey, countries of the Persian Gulf, China, South Korea and the U.S. Many U.S. states have growing communities of Uzbeks, Tajiks, Kyrgyz and other natives of the region. Uzbeks are the largest ethno-provenance group of 50,500 people. The counts for Kazakhstan natives were 24,000 people, while other ethnic groups were not shown separately (Census Bureau, 2013).

This chapter theorizes experiences of Central Asian transnational migrants through the concept of embodiment. The phenomenological framework of embodiment addresses the immediacy of "being-in-the-world" (Csordas, 1999), or making sense of the world in the process of interacting with it with the means of body. Subjective experience, transmitted through the body, influences not only immediacy of a person and his/her inner world, but provides social outcomes. The framework of embodiment helps to conceptualize movers' presence in a new place and their complex relationships with the new social environment, when migrants re-develop their empirical, existential and social selves in the place of destination. Transnational migration has implications for the physical and psychological well-being of migrants, which can be also addressed through the framework of embodiment.

This chapter builds upon ethnographic data from Russia, Tajikistan and the U.S., and discusses perceptions of insecurity and stress among Central Asian migrants in the first part. The second part of the chapter addresses agency of migrants. This helps to introduce the complexity of embodiment: although different modalities in immigrants' bodily immediacy in a new location are intertwined and could be experienced at the same time, their effect may vary with duration of stay. The framework of embodiment helps to better understand gendered responses to transnational migration, and implications for well-being of Central Asian migrants in the new destinations.

Background: Embodiment and Its Implication for Migration Studies

The concept of body has been developed by anthropologists since the early 1970s. Thomas Csordas notes: "Anthropologists with interests ranging across medical and psychological anthropology, the anthropology of space, material culture, practice theory, performance theory, critical theory and even cognitive anthropology have problematized the body" (Csordas, 1994:1). He argues that the phenomenological standpoint allows to capture the sense of existential immediacy and proposes looking at the body from perspective of "being-in-the-world" (Csordas, 1999:10). That helps to overcome the problem of objectification of the body and introduce methodological approach for the concept of embodiment: "If embodiment is an existential condition in which the body is a subjective source or intersubjective ground of experience, then studies under the rubric of embodiment are not "about" the body per se. Instead, they are about culture and experience insofar as these could be understood from the standpoint of bodily being-in-the-world" (Csordas, 1999: 144).

The phenomenological paradigm helps to explain how people experience their body most of the time, and go beyond the binary of the body and mind. Joona Taipale notes that we never experience ourselves as disembodied minds that are in contact with things and other people only in a mediated manner, through a body (Taipale, 2014: 4). The combination of the core concept of phenomenology - phenomena that appear in acts of consciousness - with bodily experience as existential knowledge provides us with the new framework to speak about people's making of their self in everyday life. The framework of embodiment refers to the assumption that thoughts, feelings, and behaviours are grounded in sensory experiences and bodily states (Meier et al. 2012:2).

The literature on embodiment of migration is relatively small. Feminist anthropology argues that the body is a theoretically powerful standpoint from which to examine migration, and it focuses analytical attention on embodied subjectivities and the roles of migrant bodies in producing space and place (Silvey, 2005:142). Notwithstanding considerable amount of works in the this field, feminist perspective imposes some limitations on conceptualizing embodiment, which is seen through the complex reading of gender, power, structure and agency, subjugation and cultural struggle; more broadly-spatialized power relations (Silvey, 2005:143).

Critiques of feminist approaches indicate that "research in the body" should not necessarily focus on power relationships; we need to rather pay attention to performative bodily practices that contribute to organize and refine the self in the society (Mahmood, 2012). Mahmood critiques the concept of habitus that Bourdieu defines as a "system of durable, transportable dispositions, structured structures predisposed to function as structuring structures, that is, as principles which generate and organize practices and representations" (Bourdieu 1990:53). Bodily practices are a fundamental component of habitus since they pass down directly without being reflected upon by the conscious mind: "The child mimics other people's actions rather than 'models'. Body hexis speaks directly to the motor function, in the form of a pattern of postures that is both individual and systematic, being bound up with a whole system of objects, and charged with a host of special meanings and values (Bourdieu 1990:72, 74).

Mahmood notes that habitus structures the individual's practices; but at the same time is challenged and continually constructed due to conscious efforts of an individual, leaving room for an agency as productive force (Mahmood, 2012). This theoretical model is useful for investigating experiences of Central Asian migrants. This chapter builds upon the concept of embodiment to capture the state of "being-in-the-world" that immigrants simultaneously experience and construct while re-developing their empirical and existential selves in the new environment.

Data and Methods

This chapter builds upon the ethnographic data from four studies of Central Asian transnational migrants[1]. Two studies of female international immigrants from Central Asia were conducted in Russia in 2010 and 2012-2013. The sample size was 224 respondents in the first survey, and 941 respondents in the second survey (including control group). The 2010 survey was conducted in Moscow; the 2012-2013 survey was conducted in Moscow and two other major urban centers of Russia: Novosibirsk and Ekaterinburg. The surveys used the same methodological approach to study three ethno-provenance groups of female migrants (Kyrgyz, Tajik and Uzbek, aged 18-40) and the control group of native Russian-born women of the same age and occupation.

[1] Partial support from the Mershon Center for International Security Studies, Ohio State University; Joint Grant from NIH/NICHD and the Russian Foundation for Basic Research. Grant #R21HD078201; NIH/NICHD, Administrative supplement to Grant #R01 HD058365; and Seed Grant Program, Arizona State University, T. Denny Sanford School of Social and Family Dynamics is gratefully acknowledged.

Because the vast majority of female Central Asian migrants work in eateries (mainly as waitresses and cleaners), semi-formal produce and clothing bazaars (as stall owners and/or vendors), and formal retail and grocery stores (mainly as sales clerks and cleaners), the survey focused on migrants working in these industries. To sample women working in eateries and formal retail, a time-location approach was used; random-walk algorithm was used to sample respondents as the bazaars.

The studies collected both quantitative and qualitative data, and focused on behavioural risks of HIV/ STD risks among Central Asian female migrants in the Russia. The survey questionnaire included questions on respondents' ethno-cultural and socioeconomic background, migration history and experiences, family life, sexual behaviour and partnerships, perceptions of HIV/STI risks and actions taken to reduce them among other questions. In-depth interviews were conducted with a subsample of respondents, and allowed to get a nuanced account of women's experiences of transnational migration. The interviews were transcribed and coded for the qualitative analysis.

This chapter also includes excerpts from a pilot online survey, conducted in 2014. Open-ended questions prompted participants to share their bodily experience in regard to their transnational relocation. Respondents included male and female natives of Russia, Kyrgyzstan and Ukraine, who moved within their countries (internal migration) or abroad (Montenegro, Cyprus, and the U.S.). Though relatively small-scale (N=14), the survey provides important insights for discussion of embodiment in this chapter. Finally, the chapter builds upon the ethnographic research among Central Asian migrants in New York City in 2015.

Central Asians in Russia: unwelcome bodies

Settlement in the country of destination, either temporary or permanent, presents migrants with different challenges and compels them to look for solutions. Central Asian immigrants navigate their way in the new environment and deal with the multiple dimensions of human insecurity. No homeownership, high rent and limited ability to secure high- or middle-income jobs create uncertainty in the future. Discrimination and financial instability becomes one of the major concerns in Russia. Different migration policies in the countries of destination and switching modalities of legality/ illegality constrain social mobility of the movers. Multiple modalities of insecurity cause stress and negatively influence migrants' health and well-being. Stressful experiences become physically embodied (Castaneda, 2010; Castaneda et al., 2015; Schneiderman et al., 2005).

Constant stress produces a "tear and wear" effect on migrants' bodies, altering physical capacities and increasing the risk of mental health problems (Arbona et al., 2010, Bhugra, 2005; Gonzales et al. 2013). Such problems as headaches and muscle tension are often directly caused by the bodily responses that accompany stress (Colingwood, 2007). Gendered relations of power in Russia and Central Asia make women migrants especially vulnerable in the context of marginalization and exclusion (Agadjanian and Zotova, 2014).

Stress takes many forms: cultural, mental and physical. Mobility, settlement and reception create opportunities but also bring challenges and problems ranging from discriminatory practices experienced directly and second hand, to stress and health challenges that are intensified by experiences of discrimination (Castaneda et al., 2015; Castaneda, 2010; Shishegar et al., 2015; Cohen and Crews, 2014). Central Asian migrants in Russia are collectively marginalized due to phenotype, limited Russian language proficiency and migration experience (Reeves 2012; Reeves 2013a; Reeves 20013b; Regamey, 2010).

Casanova and Jafar note that while globalization has facilitated movement of bodies from one place to another, not all bodies are welcomed equally and not all practices are considered acceptable (2013: xvii-xviii). Attitudes to Central Asian migrants in Russia can be viewed as an example of "unwelcome bodies". Experienced rejection and often aggression towards Central Asian natives are deeply embodied in corporeal reactions. Moreover, emotional and physical stress produces significant social outcomes, inducing disagreement and tension in relationships of spouses, friends and relatives. A Kyrgyz respondent talks about stress and family dynamics:

> *Since the very early days, from the first minute of being in Russia, I am strained. My body and my nerves are always tense, because someone might offend you at any moment; push or hit; and you are always mentally ready for it. Therefore, a lot of immigrants, specifically among my friends, start drinking hard. That is because this voltage must be resolved somehow. I witnessed a lot of such cases. I know a lot of couples who divorced after living in Russia. It is due to constant discontent, frustration, humiliation that lack of understanding and mutual insults outbreak.*

Bodily tense is exacerbated by living conditions. Married couples and individuals, male and female, young and adult movers have to pack themselves into crowded apartments to reduce their monthly expenses.

Results of the 2010 study showed that mean number of people sharing an apartment with a respondent was 14.7 for Kyrgyz, 5.3 for Tajik and 5.6 people for Uzbek respondents accordingly. The mean for all three groups of respondents was 8.5 people in an apartment (Agadjanian and Zotova, 2011).

Women noted the transformative and usually destructive effects of the sociocultural environment as well as the economic pressures of life in Russia on their morals and relationships. In a big city with generally liberal mores, relatively high incomes, and numerous opportunities for sexual relationships, immigrants' marital unions come under considerable strain. Perceived stress and hardships do not only strain marriages and relationships but might also expose migrants to the risk of sexually transmitted diseases (Zotova and Agadjanian, 2014; Weine et al., 2008). The tensions introduced by city life may amplify the potential for rupture built into traditional marriages, which often are arranged by relatives and lack romantic and emotional attachment between the wife and the husband. A Kyrgyz respondent notes (2012-2013 survey data, Moscow):

> *I see a lot of my countrywomen; they come here, young, and change right away. They change, they probably think that it's far, it's in Moscow, no one will see, no one will hear, and they... become dissolute and vulgar... they don't behave this way back home... At home, [all the norms] are followed... And the married ones change a lot too. Their husbands stay there [in the home country], and they drink, smoke, and sleep around a lot. If they were from the city, they wouldn't do that. But it is those who come from mountainous villages, from regions, and think that everything is permitted to them. If Russians do that, then it is ok for them to do that too... Those who come here with husbands, 50-60% divorce after living in Moscow. It is because of living conditions, I think, because there is no place to talk, to interact normally, no place to sleep [i.e., to have sex]. That's why marriages fall apart.*

Home as a symbolic shelter, a welcoming place where an individual can recover and rest after difficulties he meets in the outer world, does not exist in the immediate experience of Central Asian immigrants in Russia. It would require mover of any ethnic ancestry a lot of effort to cope with this stress of living together 10-15 strangers, not Central Asians alone. Attitudes to public and private space in Muslim Central Asia are very different from the conditions that migrants face in the country of destination. In Central Asia households mainly include the space inside the outer walls of the courtyard. The walls of *havlya* (courtyard) are both literal and symbolic borders of private and public space. Furthermore, cultural traditions of inhabitants of Central Asia presuppose attitudes to women. Women's movements outside the private space of the household are restricted or controlled by husband or male relatives; in some regions of Central Asia inner territory of the household is also zoned into male and female areas (Akiner, 1997; Edgar, 2006; Zanca, 2007). A significant part of male and female Central Asian immigrants originate from urban settings where gendered zoning of space is less pronounced. However, thinking along gender lines makes Central Asian migrants feel uncomfortable in the situation of forced coexistence with strange males and females.

Perceived stress is embodied through facial expressions and movement in public spaces. One could observe significant changes in the way Central Asian migrants behave in the public spaces in Russia: individuals and groups are reserved and quiet in public transport, administrative offices, health care centers, work facilities and other places. A female mover from Uzbekistan (ethnic Russian) points out (2014 survey data):

> *It took me a long time to get rid of the habit of smiling in public places: local Russian population would look at me in great surprise.*

This social mimicry is also fueled by the normative code of facial expression and behavior of local Russian population. Research papers discuss emotional restraint of Russians (see, for instance, Wierzbicka, 1999; Matsumoto, 2013). That is further reinforced by economic hardships and challenges that the majority of population face on a daily basis. These pressures are reflected in facial expressions: many outsiders report of Russian people as closed and non-smiling. This social context shapes Central Asian immigrants' bodily posture, motion and mimics. Where everyone is restrained, they are restrained to a greater extent; ready to side-glances, open discussion of them as unwelcome intruders, Central Asian immigrants carefully avoid eye contact and seemingly petrify.

Across the Ocean: New Expectations and Challenges

Russia and Central Asian countries are relatively close; and millions of migrants were able to establish strong transnational networks, which connect communities of origin and destination. Migrants' decisions are framed around expectations and social practices around emerging culture of migration. Massey defines it as a situation when "migration becomes deeply ingrained into the repertoire of people's behaviors, and values associated with migration become part of the community's values" (Massey et al., 1993: 452-53). The culture of migration identifies the abilities, limits and needs of the mover, as well as the cultural traditions and social practices; they frame abilities to move and limitations on movement through time (Cohen and Sirkeci, 2011: 13-14). Shifting consumption patterns and households' dependency on the migrants' earnings define expectations around remittances. Gendered relations of power place a double burden on women migrants in Russia. Those who follow their husbands or male relatives to a new country, often have to meet a variety of obligations. Women need to support family members in the country of origin, provide care to husbands and male relatives in Russia (cook and wash), as well as maintain their jobs and cope with long hours, discrimination in the work place and low wages.

The context of transnational connections and expectations is different for Central Asian migrants who travel overseas to settle in the Western countries. For instance, migration to the US is still relatively new; and remittances from the movers in these new destinations are irregular. It is the value of movement to the U.S. itself, rather than expectations around remittances that transform statuses for household members who are left-behind (Zotova and Cohen, 2016). Central Asian migrants in the U.S. and other Western countries navigate their way in the new environment and deal with the multiple dimensions of human insecurity; which include high rent, job insecurity, language barriers, and uncertainty in the future. Financial instability becomes one of the major concerns. Emerging insecurities are balanced by a number of mitigating factors. Phenotypic characteristics of Central Asian migrants and diversity of American urban centers facilitate integration of the newcomers. Large body of literature discusses racialization processes of immigrants in the American context (Alba, 2005; Bean et al., 2013). However, the position of Central Asian migrants on the "white side" of the colour line creates a positive effect. Skin colour and hair texture do not allow to visually distinguish them from other diverse populations; and cause racialization and exclusion, as it happens in Russia. This gives women migrants in the U.S. a larger choice of jobs, which range from low paid entry level positions in elderly and child care, bars and restaurants to graduate students and skilled professionals.

Differences in the context of reception and the size of networks define gendered trajectories for Central Asian migrants in Russia and the U.S. Parents are less likely to allow young single women to undertake a faraway trip across the ocean to the U.S. While social networks of Central Asian migrants only start to emerge in the North America, families and kin have to deal with uncertainty and fear when prospective women migrants reveal their plans. Therefore it takes single women migrants much more personal strength to convince parents to allow them to travel to the U.S. Most often, the initial plans only include a short trip for a Work-and Travel program and several months-long English language courses. However, once in the U.S., the daring young women continue to study language or look for a job, while searching the ways to adjust their legal status (Zotova and Cohen, 2016).

Gendered expectations around normative behaviour shape different trajectories for young male migrants from Central Asia in the U.S. While decision making is easier for them, men have might have fewer opportunities available for them upon arrival. When men follow gendered networks they might be limited to low-end service jobs. In a situation when fewer resources are available through social networks, compared with Russia, Central Asian women in the U.S. are likely to communicate across ethnic lines in search of jobs, accommodation, and support.

When married couples migrate together to settle in the U.S. as permanent residents they initially face the same problems as single migrants and experience hard living and working conditions, job insecurity, hardships and stress. At the same time, marriage becomes the space where gender roles and expectations are negotiated and contested in the migration setting (Hondagneo-Sotelo, 1994; Mahler, 2001; Hirsh, 2003). Cross-national scholarship in anthropology point at reconstitution of gender norms in a migration setting, associated with the entrance of women into the labor market and their increased earnings; and new configurations of gendered labor in the migrants' families (Brettell, 2003; Hirsch 2003; Hondagneo-Sotelo, 1994; Brettell, 2015). Central Asian families are no exception to these processes. Marriages are embedded within complex relations to kin, identity and place. As such, marriage works as a cultural marker that allows migrants to rethink who they are and construct identities in the new place. Families become the place where gender relations and norms are contested, which might cause conflicts, severe relationships and even lead to separation of partners.

Settlement in the environment with more relaxed gender norms provide Central Asian women with new opportunities as well. Hirsch (2003) notes that in the context of Mexican migration to the U.S. gendered attitudes to public spaced tend to reverse. Men no longer "own the street" as they do in Mexico. Women, on the other hand, navigate the public space more freely while commuting to work, shopping, going to community meetings and the like. Hirsch's argument holds true for Central Asian women migrants in Russia. Women are less often stopped and harassed by the police compared with their male counterparts. Women migrants have a wider choice of jobs in retail and service; and can enter the private spaces of native residents' homes when working as concierge, home attendants, maids or baby sitters. Brettell (2003) indicates a similar trend among Portuguese migrants in France. Compared with their communities of origin, single or divorced Central Asian women also enjoy more freedom to engage in intimate and sexual relationships, quit relationships and look for new partners at their will.

Agency: The World under Construction

When people cross borders, they do not leave behind their beliefs about bodies or habitual embodied practices (Casanova and Jafar, 2013: xi). Transnational migrants need to balance left behind families and kin, social obligations, and necessity to remit. Material conditions shape the life of movers in the new environment as well, restricting their agency. Cultural practices of Central Asia continue to inform behaviour of migrants in a new environment. However, the immediate experiences of migrants, daily interactions with unfamiliar objects, shapes, tastes and smells contribute to embodiment of migration and help newcomers to re-construct their social and cultural world along the new lines. The framework of embodiment allows investigating construction of the new meanings and practices, shaped by the agency.

The process of getting accustomed to a new environment resembles the stages that an individual passes in his development: this is the experience of constructing the world around oneself. At first it is a narrow one-dimensional circle within the reach of a child's hand, later of a turn and a crawl, then with upright position and ability to walk the child adds new dimensions to this expanding personal universe. The inclusion in social relations and space-making, exercised by the movers, follows a similar path. For instance, when recent arrivals from Central Asian countries master the urban space in Russia, they form personal ties in the new environment, and develop conceptions about reality, that had been previously alien to them. They construct their own mental map of the place where they settle (Zotova and Agadjanian, 2014). Brednikova and Tkach note that when changing their place of residence, immigrants do not simply move from one population center to another, they also reshape the space encompassed by their lives and significantly expand the boundaries of their day-to-day reality. Central Asian movers gradually acquire the city: "Easily swapping jobs and carrying their home in a box with them, women move around the city, gradually assimilating it and appropriating it [...]. Their city is structured exclusively around the Metro map. Metro stations become little centers which accumulate space around themselves." (Brednikova and Tkach, 2010: 72-73, 86).

Experience of an interviewer from Samarkand (Uzbekistan), who participated in the survey of 2010, helps to better understand space-making in the new urban setting. While developing time-location sampling frame for the project, we used the map of the Moscow Subway. Each of the studied ethnic groups was allocated the two longest Metro lines, and then the stations along these lines were re-ordered at random. As a result, the interviewers had to do a great deal of travelling around the city, assimilating the space and exploring regions far from the city centre that were new to them. Immediately prior to being introduced and beginning work on the project, Aziza had spent no more than a month in Moscow, arriving in the city shortly after her wedding. Her husband had been working and living in Moscow for several years, but to the young woman the city was entirely new and unfamiliar; she only knew the small area around her home. As work on the project progressed, she assimilated the city, spending time around Metro stations in regions all over Moscow. This experience was recounted with pride by Aziza to her relatives, who found her new knowledge surprising. They commented that there was a whole set of regions in the city where they had never been, although they had been living in Moscow for some considerable time (Zotova and Agadjanian, 2014).

The gradual construction of space goes together with the mental representation of location and distances. In the situation of relocation customary geographical ideas of one's position in a space lose their meaning, shuffling previously so solid notions of "here" and "there"; "east" and "west". With that the dimensions of the known world become blurred and confused, especially in case of crossing the ocean to a different continent. Using probably the best literary expression, given by Alice in Wonderland, getting into the world of antipodes, in a place "where everyone goes upside down" (Carroll 1865), could take the ground from under the new mover's feet. The bodily feeling of how things were "there" and how different is "here" in the new surroundings creates and enforces perception of drastic changes in the migrants' lives. Perceived stress is closely connected to spatial cognition. Henrich and McElreath note that "cultural evolution of linguistic system, and associated cultural routines, for discussing and dealing with space and orientation influences our non-linguistic spatial cognition" (Henrich and McElreath, 2007: 567). Therefore the new environment with a different linguistic system can produce significant shifts in spatial cognition. Increased duration of stay with accommodation to the new cultural environment helps to adjust the notions of "here" and "there" to the new location. Composing the new personal and social world includes acquiring a more stable position on the ground, with reconsidered locations and landmarks. While reflecting on their experience of finding jobs and securing income in Russia as well as New York City, Central Asian migrants use the recurrent narrative. They use the phrase "We got back to our feet" to indicate that they eventually managed to cope with the initial hardships of relocation.

Out of movers' different relations with the new environment, agency could produce the most powerful effect on interactions with materiality. In a number of material objects that could be discussed in the context of embodiment, clothing can comprise the broadest range of meanings. It is the meeting place of conscious and unconscious; and the showcase of exercised agency. Dressing style in the new location can significantly differ from that in the place of origin. Female informants (2014 survey data), who moved to the U.S. from Russia, noted how they distinguished from the local population at first, dressing too smart, but later got used to a more simplistic code.

Central Asian women migrants have more changes in clothing style than men. That might be explained by the changing perceptions of selves and new resources that they get in the new environment. Central Asian women describe their experiences by a similar narrative:

> *That is Russia; here it's different; there are other rules here; you need to dress like a Russian; you can't not dress here like you do back home; you should not stand out...*

This specific kind of a social mimicry is informed by xenophobia in the Russian society. Upon relocation to Russia Central Asian migrants experience lots of hardships, and are not willing to make their appearance an additional factor of exclusion. Due to these, Central Asian women in a traditional costume (a dress made of bright fabric and pants) can be rarely seen on the streets of Russian cities. However, moving out of highly regulated social world of Central Asia, its natives acquire new degree of personal agency. It can be seen in the choice of clothes, haircut and dyed hair, makeup and even jewelry. In an effort to "dress like a Russian" female immigrants from Central Asia sometimes hit the other extreme. A 21-year old Kyrgyz interviewer in 2010 study has lived in Russia since childhood, and often provides advice and guidance to newcomers. She reflects on her friends' experiences:

They begin to dress differently. When they come to Moscow, I tell them – you need to dress differently, here you cannot wear a long dress and a headscarf. I change clothes for them, and say that they should dress in a more open style. They immediately put on mini-skirts, where everything is on display [legs]. Immediately, mind you, and they have only just arrived in long dresses [from Kyrgyzstan]. They let their hair down, put on a mini-dress and nylon tights. I saw a friend yesterday; she was in nylon tights, a really short skirt. She has a big breast, but she had on a really thin blouse on; she could hardly button it up. My god, what did she look like? And it was freezing and snowing! Anyway, she only got here a month ago."

Relocation changes bodily practices; and modalities of embodiment are larger than stress responses, discussed in the previous chapter. Embodiment of migration for Central Asian movers resolves some conflicts through the agency, and creates new conflicts at the same time. Central Asian cultural traditions emphasize social control, where individual decisions subjugate to decisions of parents, elder relatives and norms of the community. Embodied discomfort and suffering caused by crowded living conditions and hostile environment in Russia, as well as financial instability and sometimes problematic legal status in the U.S. are balanced by the resolution of other tensions, caused by gendered relations of power in the home countries. Central Asian migrants enjoy more freedom to engage in intimate relationships and look for new partners at their will. A Kyrgyz respondent puts it like this:

My husband was my first man. When I divorced, I had not one and two, but many more partners. Here [in Russia] I began to meet with men that I fancied.

This statement emphasizes one of the core components of Central Asian migrants' experiences in the new environment, which is the larger agency and ability to do what they like in regards to their bodies (Farnell, 1999). As such, Central Asian migrants master new social environments with the means of agency. They discover new pleasures and opportunities that shift patterns of romantic and sexual behaviour. It would be hard to argue that emerging social world of Central Asian immigrants in the places of destination is centered on pleasures. They face hard work, crowded living conditions, high level of xenophobia in Russian society, problematic legal status and financial insecurity in the U.S., and other hardships. However, the agency exercised through their bodies produces significant changes in immigrants' immediacy.

Conclusion

This chapter discusses transnational migration from Central Asia and employs the theoretical framework of embodiment to address subjective experiences of migrants. The phenomenological framework provides important insights for migration theories, linking interpretive anthropological methods to broader social outcomes of migration. The concept of embodiment provides migration researchers with important analytical tools that allow to capture the immediacy of "being-in-the-world", and explore how movers navigate their new social environments. The framework of embodiment helps to better understand gendered responses to transnational migration, and implications for well-being of Central Asian migrants in the new destinations.

The focus on the bodies of people that move, suffer and discover the new world in the process of relocation helps to understand transnational migration as dynamically embodied action (Farnell, 1999:341). The inquiry into gendered pathways of Central Asian migrants across the world can draw attention to a variety of topics: family and intergenerational dynamics, experiences of settlement in a different socio-cultural context, access to resources, opportunities and networks in the countries of destination and more. Central Asian migrants navigate their way in the new countries, work, and study, start new families or exit the relationships, raise children, become permanent residents or eventually return home. While settling in the countries of destination Central Asian migrants redefine cultural values; and renegotiate gender roles in the new context. Gendered trajectories of settlement make a framework for better understanding of opportunities, continuity and change as Central Asian migrants maintain and reinvent their identities in the new setting.

The framework of embodiment helps to conceptualize movers' presence in a new place and their complex relationships with the new social environment, when migrants re-develop their empirical, existential and social selves in the place of destination.

Proposed framework for understanding experiences of Central Asian migrants has some limitations as well. While addressing the immediacy of the individuals' "being-in-the-world", it might be harder to apply the concept of embodiment for broader generalizations. However, the concept of embodiment of migration can produce important insights into understanding the implications of migration for the physical and psychological well-being of movers. Cultural background and religious affiliation shape different responses to stressful situations among various groups of immigrants. Attention to gendered stress responses might be helpful for further research on physical and psychological well-being of migrants, including general health and mental health outcomes. Mahler and Pessar argue for "bringing gender in" migration studies and note: "Ethnography stresses a holistic and contextual approach that is particularly useful for examining complex concepts and practices such as relations between men and women" (Mahler and Pessar, 2006: 31). Combining phenomenology of embodiment with the feminist ethnography has a potential of pushing migration theories and better understanding experiences of individuals and their complex interactions with the new social world that they find themselves in.

References

Abashin, S. (2014). Migration from Central Asia to Russia in the New Model of World Order. *Russian Politics & Law,* 52 (6): 8-23.

Agadjanian V. and Zotova, N. (2014). Immigration and HIV risks: Central Asian female Migrants in the Russian Federation. *Demographic Review,* 1 (2): 85-109 (in Russian).

Agadjanian, Victor, and Natalia Zotova. 2011. Social Vulnerability and Sexual Risks of Female Migrants from Central Asia in Moscow. *Demoscope Weekly* 465-466 (May 2-22). Accessed from http://demoscope.ru/weekly/2011/0465/analit02.php#_FNR_1 (in Russian)

Akiner, S. (1997). "Between tradition and modernity - the dilemma facing contemporary Central Asian women". In *Post Soviet Women: From the Baltic to Central Asia.* M. Buckley (ed.). Cambridge: Cambridge University Press, pp. 261-304.

Alba, R. (2005). Bright vs. blurred boundaries: Second generation assimilation and exclusion in France, Germany, and the United States. *Ethnic and Racial Studies,* 28 (1): 20-49.

Arbona, C. (2010). Acculturative Stress among documented and undocumented Latino Immigrants in the United States. *Hispanic Journal of Behavioral Sciences,* 32 (3):362-84.

Bean, F. et al. (2013). Immigration & the color line at the beginning of the 21st century. *Dedalus,* 142 (3): 123-140.

Bhugra, D. (2005). Cultural identities and cultural congruency: A new model for evaluating mental distress in immigrants. *Acta Psychiatr Scand,* 111 (2): 84-93.

Bourdieu, P. (1990). *The Logic of Practice.* Stanford: Stanford University Press.

Brednikova, O. and Tkach, O. (2010). A home for a Nomad. *Laboratorium,* 3 (in Russian).

Carroll, L. (1865). *Alice's Adventures in Wonderland.* New York: Macmillan.

Brettell, C. and Hollifield, J. (2015). *Migration Theory. Talking Across Disciplines.* 3rd Edition. New York and London: Routledge.

Brettell, C. (2003). Anthropology and Migration. Essays on Transnationalism, Ethnicity and Identity. New York: AltaMira Press.

Casanova, E. M. and Jafar, A. (2013). "Bodies, borders and the other: An introduction". In *Bodies Without Borders*. E. M. de Casanova and A. Jafar (eds.). New York: Palgrave Macmillan, pp. ix-xxi.

Castañeda, H. (2010). Im/migration and health: conceptual, methodological, and theoretical propositions for applied anthropology. *Napa Bulletin*, 34: 6-27.

Castañeda, H. et al. (2015). Immigration as a Social Determinant of Health. *Annual Review of Public Health*, 36: 1.1-1.18.

Collingwood, J. (2007). The Physical Effects of Long-Term Stress. *Psych Central*. Accessed from http://psychcentral.com/lib/the-physical-effects-of-long-term-stress/000935 on 24 October 2014.

Csordas, T. (1999). "Embodiment and cultural phenomenology". In *Perspectives on Embodiment. The Intersections of Nature and Culture*. G. Weiss and H. F. Haber (eds.). New York and London: Routledge.

Csordas, T. (1994). "Introduction: the body as representation and being-in-the-world". In *Embodiment and Experience. The Existential Ground of Culture and Self*. T. J. Csordas (ed.). Cambridge: Cambridge University Press.

Cohen, J. H. and Crews, D. E. (2014). Comparing Physiological and Social Stressors among Latino Immigrants to Columbus, Ohio. Paper presented at the Annual Meeting of the American Anthropological Association, Washington, DC.

Cohen, J. H. and Sirkeci, İ. (2011). *Cultures of Migration. The Global Nature of Contemporary Mobility*. Austin: University of Texas Press.

Collingwood, J. (2007). The Physical Effects of Long-Term Stress. *Psych Central*.

Edgar, A. L. (2006). Bolshevism, patriarchy and the nation: the Soviet 'emancipation' of Muslim women in pan-Islamic perspective. *Slavic Review*, 65: 252-72.

Farnell, B. (1999). Moving bodies, acting selves. *Annual Review of Anthropology*, 28: 341-73.

Gonzales, R. G., Suárez-Orozco, C. and Dedios-Sanguineti, M. C. (2013). No place to belong. Contextualizing concepts of mental health among undocumented immigrant youth in the United States. *American Behavioral Scientist*, 57 (8): 1174-1199.

Heleniak, T. (2008). "An overview of migration in the Post-Soviet space". In *Migration, Homeland and Belonging in Eurasia*. C. Buckley and B. Ruble (eds.). Washington, DC: Woodrow Wilson Center and Johns Hopkins University PresS, pp. 29-67.

Henrich, J. and McElreath, R. (2007). "Dual-inheritance theory: the evolution of human cultural capacities and cultural evolution". In *The Oxford Handbook of Evolutionary Psychology*. L. Barrett and R. Dunbar (eds.). Oxford: Oxford University Press, pp. 555-70.

Hirsch, J. (2003). A Courtship after Marriage: Sexuality and Love in Mexican Transnational Families. Berkeley: University of California Press.

Hondagneo-Sotelo, P. (1994). *Gendered Transitions. Mexicans Experiences of Immigration*. Berkeley: University of California Press.

Mahler, S. J. (2001). Transnational relationships: The struggle to communicate across borders. *Identities: Global Studies in Culture and Power*, 7 (4): 583-619.

Mahmood, S. (2012). *Politics of Piety. The Islamic Revival and the Feminist Subject.* Reissue with a new preface. Princeton and Oxford: Princeton University Press.

Massey, D. et al. (1993). Theories of international migration: A review and appraisal. *Population and Development Review,* 19 (3): 431-466.

Matsumoto, D., Frank, M. G. and Hwang, H. (2103). *Nonverbal Communication. Science and Applications. D.* Matsumoto, M. G. Frank and H. Hwang (eds.). Thousand Oaks: SAGE publications.

Ministry of Internal Affairs of the Russian Federation (MIARF). (2016). Some migration indicators in the Russian Federation in January-September 2016. Accessed from https://xn--b1aew.xn--p1ai/Deljatelnost/statistics/migracionnaya/ item/ 8861965/ on 1 December 2016.

Meier, B., Schnall, S., Schwarz, N. and Bargh, J. A. (2012). Embodiment in social psychology. *Topics in Cognitive Science*: 1-12.

Reeves, M. (2013a). Clean fake: Authenticating documents and persons in migrant Moscow. *American Ethnologist,* 40: 508-24.

Reeves, M. (2013b). Kak stanoviatsia "chernym" v Moskve: praktiki vlasti i sushchestvovanie mitrantov v teni zakona [Becoming "Black" in Moscow: Documentary Regimes and *Migrant* Life in the Shadow of Law]. In *Grazhdanstvo i immigratsiia: kontseptual'noe, istoricheskoe i institutsional'noe izmerenie [Citizenship and Immigration: Conceptual, Historical and Institutional Dimensions].* V. Malakhov (ed.). Moscow: Russian Academy of Sciences/ Kanon+, pp. 146-77 (in Russian).

Reeves, M. (2012). Black work, green money: Remittances, ritual, and domestic economies in Southern Kyrgyzstan. *Slavic Review,* 71: 108-34.

Regamey, A. (2010). Representations of immigrants and migration policy in Russia. *Anthropologicheskiy. Forum,* 13 (in Russian).

Silvey, R. (2005). "Borders, embodiment and mobility: Feminist migration studies in geography. In *A Companion to Feminist Geography.* L. Nelson and J. Seager (eds.). Padstow: Blackwell Publishing, pp. 138-49.

Schneiderman, Neil et al. (2005). Stress and health: Psychological, behavioral, and biological determinants. *Annual Review of Clinical Psychology,* 1: 607-28.

Shishehgar et al. (2015). The impact of migration on the health status of Iranians: an integrative literature review. *BMC International Health and Human Rights:* 15-20.

Taipale, J. (2014). Phenomenology and Embodiment. Husserl and the Constitution of Subjectivity. Evanston: Northwestern University Press.

Wierzbicka, A. (1999). *Emotions across Languages and Cultures: Diversity and Universals.* Cambridge: Cambridge University Press.

United States Census Bureau. (2013). Place of Birth for the Foreign-born Population in the United States. Universe: Foreign-born Population Excluding Population Born at Sea. 2009-2013 American Community Survey 5-Year Estimates. Accessed from https://factfinder.census.gov/faces/tableservices/jsf/pages/productview.xhtml? src=bkmk on 22 January 2017.

Weine, S. et al. (2008). Unprotected Tajik male migrant workers in Moscow at risk for HIV/AIDS. *J Immigrant Minority Health,* 10: 461–468.

Zanca, R. and Sahadeo, J. (2007). *Everyday Life in Central Asia.* R. Zanca and J. Sahadeo (eds.). Bloomington: Indiana University Press.

Zotova, N. and Jeffrey H. C. (2016). Remittances and their social meaning in Tajikistan. *Remittances Review,* 1 (1): 5-16.

Chapter Four

For Love or for Papers? Sham Marriages among Turkish (Potential) Migrants and Gender Implications

Işık Kulu-Glasgow, Monika Smit and Roel Jennissen

Introduction

Under the impact of globalization and continuing migration flows to the European countries, marriage migration became an important way of immigration to these countries. The countries of the European Union (EU) apply restrictive marriage migration policies towards non-EU citizens. In addition to the implementation of stricter requirements transnational couples have to fulfil (e.g., regarding income and pre-integration of the immigrating partner even before migration), there has been increasing political attention to combat sham marriages. At the request of several European countries, the European Commission recently provided a Handbook with common guidelines to identify and combat sham marriages (COM/2014/284). According to the Handbook and the EU-directive that describes the rights of EU-citizens and their family members regarding their free movement within the EU (2004/38/EG), a marriage is considered to be sham[1] if its *sole* purpose is to gain a residence permit for the potential immigrant partner.[2] Such marriages are regarded as a means to enter and reside in Europe illegally (Council of the European Union, 2012), considered to be fraud, and seen as an abuse of immigration policy (2004/38/EG). The numbers on identified or suspected sham marriages in European countries – if available at all - not only vary considerably but are

---

[1] The EU-directive uses the term 'marriage of convenience', but in this chapter we prefer the term 'sham marriage' for narrative purposes.

[2] According to the EU-guidelines, a marriage cannot be considered as sham simply because it brings an immigration advantage, or any other advantage (COM/2009/313).

---

often incomparable as they are based on different indicators. However, there is evidence that an overwhelming majority of migration marriages are genuine. According to a study by Pöyry (2010), in 2009 only a little over 2% of all applications for family reunification in Norway were rejected due to suspicions of a sham marriage. The same study suggests that the numbers are lower in Denmark, and are not expected to exceed 5% in Sweden.

In the contemporary world, in general it is women who migrate more often in connection with marriage. This difference with male migration has been associated with global hypergamy (the desire for an 'upward movement') (Constable, 2005).[3] There is hardly any evidence in the literature on whether there are also gender differences in the frequency of sham marriages in Europe. However, evaluation of marriage migration applications by immigration authorities seem to be based on a general impression that it is usually women who conduct sham marriages with (irregular) migrant men (cf. Tamburlini, 2014). Several studies suggest that there is a gender bias in the way immigration authorities check marriage-migration applications to determine whether a marriage is 'for love or for papers'[4]. According to De Hart (2000, 2001), due to suspicions of a sham marriage and the idea that Dutch women are being deceived by migrant men, migration marriages between Dutch female sponsors and male migrants were more often checked by the immigration authorities than those between Dutch men and female migrants. Evidence from research in Germany, Italy (Shevtsova, 2013), Norway (Mühleisen et al. 2012) and Austria (Messinger, 2013) also indicates that applications by women with foreign partners are more likely to be checked on the 'genuineness' of the relationship by the immigration authorities than applications by men with foreign partners. Immigration authorities seem to consider women marrying immigrant men naive, vulnerable, or reckless (Wray, 2006).

According to Tamburlini (2014) sham marriages are seen as a threat to security and family values and women as 'potentially vulnerable', in need to be safeguarded within the context of state control of undocumented migrants. Similarly, Carver (2016) argues that in connection to

---

[3] Constable (2005) stresses that women do not always move upwards socio-economically as a result of migration; they are not necessarily poor or categorically marry men who are at a higher socio-economic position.

[4] We use the 'love or papers' dichotomy to emphasize the contrast between sham relationships and genuine ones, being fully aware of the fact that not all genuine relationships need to be based on love.

increasingly restrictive marriage migration policies and increasing feelings of national identity, the nation states see women as 'disabled' citizens for whom they must act as a responsible patriarch to protect them from 'others': migrants.

Within this 'rescue narrative' (cf. Bracke, 2012) of the states, women are seen as (potential) victims of unlawful, fraudulent sham marriages. Knowledge on the frequency and nature of Turkish sham marriages[5] in Europe is very limited, but existing evidence implies that victimization is only partially true for women involved in Turkish sham marriages. According to the previously mentioned study by Pöyry, applicants from Turkey, Morocco, Vietnam and Somalia rank together as top three regarding the number of rejections based on sham marriages in Norway. Some of the cases reported concerned Turkish men marrying older Norwegian women in order to obtain residence permit (EMN, 2012; Pöyry (2010). Often, these marriages appeared to be a 'one-way marriage of convenience', meaning that the sponsoring partner believes that the relationship is genuine, while the potential partner uses it as an opportunity to obtain a residence permit (Pöyry, 2010). In this contribution we prefer the term *unilateral* sham marriages to refer to this type of marriages. Such cases were detected because the migrant in question applied for family migration immediately after his asylum application had been rejected, and filed for divorce once he had obtained a long-term residence permit or citizenship (EMN, 2012). Cases were identified where after the divorce, the man's real partner (sometimes also children) from Turkey applied for family reunification (Pöyry, 2010). There are suspicions that this pattern also exists in Denmark (Charsley and Liversage, 2013). Henriksen and Frich (2008) refer to such constructions to reunite with the real partner, as the 'Turkish trick'[6] (cited in Charsley and Liversage, 2013). These studies suggest that (elderly) native European women are sometimes indeed victims of sham marriages, initiated by Turkish men seeking legal residence for themselves and for their real families. However, there is also evidence of women being involved as active agents in *bilateral* Turkish sham marriages - cases where both partners are aware of the real purpose of the marriage: a residence permit for the migrant. Research shows that

---

[5] We use the term 'Turkish sham marriages' to refer to cases where at least one of the partners is of Turkish origin. And we use the term 'Turkish' for narrative purposes and thereby refer to all ethnic groups originating from Turkey.

[6] Similar constructions of sham marriages with the same purpose were reported among North African men (Pöyry, 2010).

Turkish migrants were involved in sham marriages with Polish sponsors in Scotland to whom they paid £3.000, but probably also took part in different ways in criminal networks that arranged such marriages in Turkey, where criminals earned £7.000 per marriage. There is no specific information about the gender of the Turkish migrants involved, but an overwhelming majority of migrants who entered into sham marriages were men and Poland was 'providing fake brides' (Polish Ministry of Interior, 2012).

In this chapter, we focus on sham marriages in the Netherlands and answer the following central questions: 1) what is the prevalence of Turkish sham marriages? 2) In which forms do these marriages manifest themselves and what are their gender implications?

Before answering these questions, we present some background information regarding the Dutch policy context and existing information on Turkish sham marriages.

The Dutch Context: Policies and Turkish Sham Marriages in the Netherlands

The Netherlands applies a restrictive marriage migration policy for non-EU migrants, including those from Turkey.[7] Turkish migrants form the largest non-western migrant group in the country, with their migration history originating in 1960s when the 'guest workers' arrived. Although there is a shift among the second-generation towards marrying a Turkish partner already living in the Netherlands (Van Huis, 2007), marriage migration is still the most common form of immigration from Turkey. Turkish marriage migrants are ranked as number one among all marriage migrants from non-EU countries.[8]

The Dutch government has been implementing measures to tackle sham marriages for the last 2.5 decades. In 1994 a specific law to combat sham marriages was introduced. In October 2012, the period after which an immigrant partner can apply for a Dutch residence permit, independent of his/her sponsoring partner, was increased from three to five years. By this latest measure the government aimed at 'decreasing the attractiveness of a sham marriage as a 'springboard' to an independent residence permit'. From

---

[7] As a result of the Association Agreement between the EU and Turkey, recently several restrictions (e.g. regarding age and civic integration) have been lifted for Turkish marriage migrants in the Netherlands.

[8] Between January 1, 2009 and June 30, 2014 17% of all applications for marriage migration from non-EU countries were submitted by Turkish (potential) migrants (Kulu-Glasgow et al., 2016).

2011 through 2014, the Dutch Immigration and Naturalisation Service (IND) implemented a project which targeted applications of non-EU migrants with partners from the EU. The project aimed at identifying possible sham marriages by conducting an individual hearing with each partner if the background characteristics and the history of the partners involved 'risk factors' for a sham marriage (such as a history of illegal stay in the country, or a previous sham marriage) (Kulu-Glasgow et al. 2016). The project was initiated as a response to a sudden increase of applications for family migration by women from eastern EU-countries and male migrant partners from non-EU countries (Van der Wolff, 2012).[9]

Despite various measures, there was a lack of concrete, representative figures over the prevalence of sham marriages. Since the end of the 1980s politicians and researchers mentioned figures ranging from 2 to 80% of all migration marriages (Kulu-Glasgow et al., 2016). An 'indicative' finding regarding the frequency of Turkish sham marriages came from the study by Van Huis and Steenhof (2013). Using national register data the authors state that after ten years of marriage, couples consisting of a first generation Turkish male migrant and a Dutch woman have the highest risks for divorce (compared to couples with a male migrant from Morocco, Surinam or the Netherlands Antilles, the three other big migrant groups in the Netherlands). The authors remark that divorce rates for marriages between Dutch women and Turkish men show a noticeable peak after four years of marriage, which may indicate the existence of sham marriages[10] (at that time a marriage migrant had to be married for three years to get an independent residence permit).

Knowledge on manifestation forms of Turkish sham marriages is also quite limited and comes mostly from research on marriage migration in general or on irregular migration. A study by Engbersen et al. (2006) presents a case of an irregular Turkish migrant who, on the advice of his niece, entered a sham marriage with a Dutch woman who agreed to this marriage for financial reasons. His brother-in-law lent him the money to pay off the 'bride'. In his study focusing on irregular Turkish migrants in the city of Rotterdam, Staring (2001) presents a case of a Turkish man who attempted to enter a sham marriage with a Surinamese woman. The 'bride' was recruited for then 10,000 guilders with the help of, among others, his sister, the Turkish neighbours and a Turkish marriage broker. However, he was deported to Turkey before the marriage took place. In these two cases of bilateral sham marriages Turkish women are not involved as partners, but they play an

---

[9] Since 2015 the approach of the project is implemented nationwide for applications of all couples consisting of partners with an EU and non-EU nationality.

[10] The same trend was observed for marriages between Dutch women and Moroccan men.

active role by acting as intermediaries in private spheres or by advising a family member to use a sham marriage as a migration strategy. According to Staring (2001) there is a fear among the Turkish community for being abused in unilateral sham marriages by irregular migrants who are seeking 'papers'. Sterckx, et al. (2014) report that such distrust also exists regarding partners 'imported' from Turkey.

Method

Data used in this chapter comes from a recent research on sham marriages by the Dutch Scientific Research and Documentation Centre (WODC) (Kulu-Glasgow et al., 2016). The study contains data from the registers of the Statistics Netherlands (CBS), which include a register with the marriages and divorces of all registered residents of the Netherlands, and data from a representative sample of applications for marriage migration obtained from the Dutch Immigration and Naturalisation Service (IND).

Firstly, the prevalence of Turkish sham marriages was estimated by following in the CBS registers all Turkish migration marriages (where both partners were Turkish) that were established between 1999 and 2008 (almost 4,000) until the end of 2013, and calculating possible divorce rates.[11] These rates were compared with those of the marriages established during the same period where both partners were second generation Turks (the control group). We expected higher divorce rates among transnational couples than among second generation couples. However, in cases of sham marriages we also expected that after three years[12] there would be a change in the *pattern* of divorces among transnational couples, compared to the second generation: less separations just before three years and a peak after that period. To eliminate the 'natural' differences in divorce rates between the two groups, the divorce-rate curve for the control group was brought to the same level as that of the transnational couples.[13] On the basis of a possible deviation of the divorce rate curve for transnational couples from that of the second generation after 3 years

---

[11] The registers include information on all types of cohabitation (marriage, registered partnership and living together) and divorces/break-ups of all registered residents of the Netherlands. In this chapter we use the term 'marriage' as this is the most common form of cohabitation among the Turkish population. The same applies to the terms 'divorce' and 'break-up'.

[12] As stated before, until October 1, 2012 it was possible to apply for an independent residence permit after three years of marriage.

[13] This is done by multiplying the monthly divorce rates of the control group by the average ratio between the divorce rates of the migrant group and the control group.

+ x months, the proportion of sham marriages in migration marriages was estimated.[14]

Secondly, the share of marriage migration applications that were rejected as sham by the Dutch Immigration and Naturalisation Service (IND) was calculated by using a representative sample of the IND files of marriage migration applications. The sample contained a total of 260 applications (respectively 130 granted and 130 rejected applications), on which the immigration authorities took a decision between January 1, 2009 and mid-June 2014. In all, 52 applications belonged to Turkish (potential) immigrants (by chance, respectively 26 granted and 26 rejected applications).[15] The shares of granted and rejected applications by Turkish migrants in the sample (both 20%) were both a good reflection of the distribution in the total population.

Thirdly, the manifestation forms of sham marriages were studied by collecting narratives from the files in the IND sample. In order to collect more qualitative information all applications of (potential) immigrants in the sample, including their possible earlier and later applications, were studied. The researchers described the situation as recorded and judged by the immigration officials, without their own perception on whether a marriage was sham or not. In addition, a limited number of interviews were held (with a Turkish healthcare provider working in a neighbourhood with a predominantly migrant population, a Turkish immigrant with Dutch nationality, and a representative of the Dutch Alien's police).

The qualitative findings we present are not meant to make any generalisations, but to investigate the nature of manifestation forms of Turkish sham marriages and their gender implications.

RESULTS

Turkish Sham Marriages: Estimated Prevalence and Rejected Applications

Figure 4.1 shows the divorce rates for Turkish migration marriages in the Netherlands and the adjusted rates for the second generation of Turkish origin, based on data from Statistics Netherlands. An estimated 2.2% of all Turkish migration marriages involved a sham relationship. This estimate almost equals

---

[14] It was assumed that in case of a sham marriage, the marriage would be dissolved within 3 years + 18 months after the wedding. This time frame was chosen because the patterns of the divorce rates of the research group and that of the control group became similar after 18 months.

[15] A variety of nationalities were represented in the sample; the most frequent origins apart from Turkish were: Moroccan, Surinamese, Ghanaian, and Chinese.

the estimate of sham marriages among all migration marriages (2.1%), is lower than the ones for the Moroccan migration marriages (3.1%) and for marriages between Sub-Saharan African men and native Dutch women (4.8%); but higher than the percentage of sham marriages between female immigrants from South-East Asia and native Dutch men (1.2%). An estimate was also made for the marriages between immigrants from English speaking, western, non-EU countries (United States, Canada, Australia and New Zealand) and native Dutch. The percentage of sham marriages in this group was zero[16] (Kulu-Glasgow et. al. 2016). As we did not expect to find any sham marriages for these couples, this analysis can be seen as a check – with a positive outcome - on the validity of the estimation method used.

Figure 4.1. Estimation of Turkish sham marriages in the Netherlands

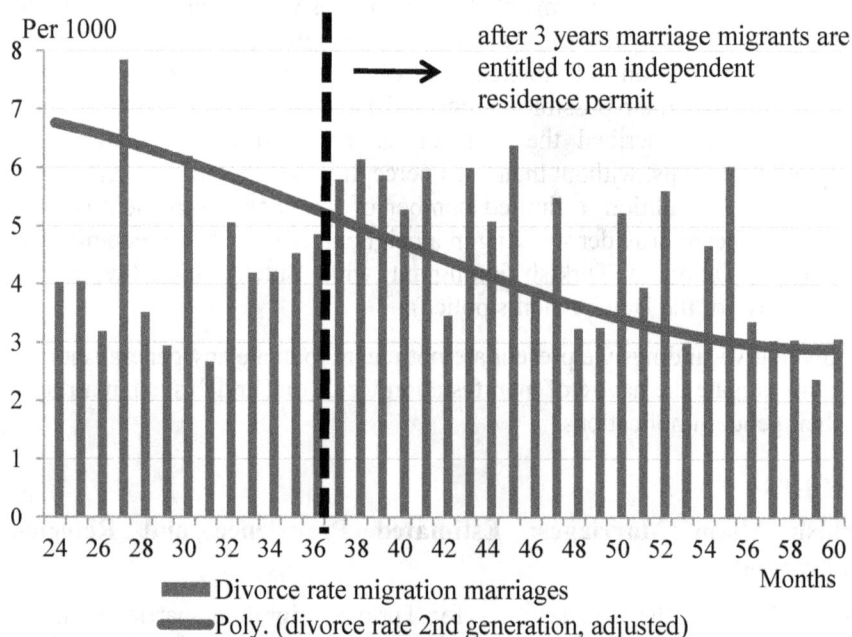

Divorce rate migration marriages
Poly. (divorce rate 2nd generation, adjusted)

The analyses of IND files shows that of all 52 applications of Turkish potential marriage migrants, two were rejected by the immigration authorities because of a sham relationship (2.7 %).[17] This is 7.7% of the applications

---

[16] The control group for the Moroccan migration marriages consisted of marriages between the second-generation Moroccan population. For the other groups under study, marriages between native Dutch served as a control group.

[17] Weighted percentage. In the total population, the percentage of granted applications of Turkish marriage migrants is almost twice as high as that of the rejected applications, while in

which were rejected in first instance. Both these percentages are lower than those for the total sample where 4% of the total applications and 12% of all rejections in first instance were rejected due to a sham marriage. Both two cases involved Turkish men and Polish women (see further).[18]

Manifestations of Turkish Sham Marriages and Their Gender Implications

As the literature suggests, Turkish sham marriages manifest themselves as bilateral or unilateral arrangements, in which different others can play a role. In this section we illustrate these manifestation forms by using information from interviews and file-analyses, focusing on the role of the women involved. We present different narratives by grouping them into bilateral and unilateral sham marriages, as it becomes clear from cases presented that these two different types of sham marriages have different gender implications for the women involved.

Bilateral Sham Marriages

The first example concerns a commercial sham marriage, arranged in personal, private settings with the help of the family.

Turkish-Dutch woman, respondent, in her fifties; talking about the experience of a close acquaintance:

"She came to the Netherlands as a 'tourist'* to visit her sister and to 'investigate her chances in the Netherlands'. She was married and had a child. Through acquaintances she found a job in horticulture and decided to stay in the Netherlands. Together with her family she came to the conclusion that entering a sham marriage was the easiest way to be able stay legally. Her brothers arranged a man with Turkish roots who would marry her for €5,000. She divorced her husband in Turkey and after getting remarried she brought her child over. She was registered at her 'husband's address but she lived at her sister's. After three years of marriage she got her residence permit and a divorce. Later she did not remarry her ex-husband with whom she had problems, but married someone else from her village and brought him over."

* *A term used by Turkish migrants in the Netherlands to refer to irregular migrants from Turkey.*

---

the sample this share is 50%. To correct for this distribution bias in the sample, a weighting factor is used when we report on the *total* number of applications.

[18] It is important to emphasize that the percentages from both sources are not comparable as: a) they do not cover the same period; b) they do not refer to exactly the same background of the couples as far as country of origin is concerned (only one or both partners of Turkish origin); and c) the estimated percentage concerns a population whose application had been granted, the percentage from the file-analyses concerns sham marriages that were discovered at the 'gate'.

In this case the Turkish woman is definitely not a victim, but an active agent who enters a sham marriage as an ultimate 'migration strategy', most probably initiated by her family members who know the ins and outs of how the Dutch system works. She uses the sham marriage not only to secure a legal residency in the Netherlands, but also as a liberating opportunity to end her apparently unsettled real marriage and choose for another partner. She was successful in her first attempt, but that is not always the case, as the next example shows in which a Turkish male migrant and two Polish female sponsors are involved:

Turkish man, late thirties
Two Polish women, both begin forties:

A Turkish man with a five years entry-ban[*] to the Netherlands, submitted an application for family migration with a Polish partner after the expiry of the ban. A year before that, he was divorced from his wife in Turkey.

During the application procedure with the first Polish partner, the couple did not meet the 'at least six months living together' criterion[**] and, according to the immigration authorities, failed to prove their 'durable and exclusive' relationship. In addition, the Polish woman, as a sponsor, failed to provide documents such as salary slips or a written labour contract to prove that she actually had the job she claimed she had. The application was rejected. The couple appealed the decision, showing a document about an appointment at the city hall to get married. The appeal was still rejected.

About a year later, the man made a second application with another Polish woman, which raised the suspicions of the immigration officials. An investigation was conducted. It was established that the couple was living at the same address but there were doubts about their relationship. According to the officials, the couple failed to be able to prove their relationship by objective means such as any photo's or a common bank account. The communication between the two was restricted, as they did not speak a common language. The nameplate at the door contained the name of the Polish sponsor and another man, with whom she did have a common bank account. The investigators had the impression that these two people had a relationship. The application was rejected on the grounds of a sham relationship, as were the subsequent appeal and higher appeal.

[*] *An entry ban can be declared on an 'unwanted alien' from non-EU countries as a result of illegal stay, criminal offences, or because of a risk for the public order or national security, usually for a maximum of five years. In that period he/she is not allowed to enter most of the EU-countries (www.judex.nl).*

[**] *One of the requirements for couples consisting of an EU-citizen and non-EU-citizen and who have an unregistered partnership.*

In this case, though it is not clear what the exact situation of these Polish sponsors was, the narratives and the progress of events suggest that these women probably acted as active agents and were paid for their services.

Information from the files indicates that a sham marriage may be used by irregular migrants as one of the several ways to try to obtain a residence permit, and also as an 'alternative route' if other strategies do not work. In one of the cases under study, a Turkish irregular, male migrant first applied for a Dutch residence permit as an entrepreneur. Before receiving the result of that application, he submitted another application for marriage migration with a Polish woman. She was a divorcee with a child, ten years older than him. During the application she had submitted a labour contract obtained from the Turkish man's employer, who also acted as a witness in the wedding, which raised the suspicions of the immigration authorities. Meanwhile his application for a residence permit as an entrepreneur was rejected, followed by the rejection of the marriage migration application. Subsequently, the couple submitted two other applications, which were also rejected. Finally, the Turkish man applied for a residence permit referring to the Turkish-EU Association Agreement.[19] The outcome of that application was not yet known yet during the file-analysis.The interview with a representative of the Dutch Alien Police reveals that some of the sham marriages between Turkish men and Polish women were not only commercial, but also took place with the involvement of criminal networks. The respondent explains how a recently identified criminal network that arranged sham marriages between Turkish men and Polish women operated.

> "The Turkish men all came from the same village in Turkey. A Turkish employment agency in the Netherlands, whose owner originated from this same community, played an important role in arranging these sham marriages by assuring that the Polish women who acted as sponsors met the income criteria*. Through some bogus labour-arrangements he made sure that these women got a quick permanent labour contract. Polish women, who were about the same age as the Turkish men, were recruited by a Polish woman. Some of these 'brides' were recruited in the Netherlands, others came from the recruiter's town in Poland.
>
> The owner of the employment agency arranged also the paper work for the legal immigration of different men, including some family members, who paid him between €15,000 and €20,000. The Polish women were promised to be paid €5,000. However, in more than one case they were defrauded and never received any money. All these Polish women were in a fragile socio-economic position: divorcees with children and debts."
>
> * *One of the requirements for marriage migration is that EU-sponsors have a job or enough financial means to support their immigrant partners from non-EU countries.*

---

[19] According to this Agreement a Turkish citizen can be entitled to a residence permit if one of the partners has worked for the last year for a company in the Netherlands and if the employer is intending to employ the person for at least another year.

The socio-economically vulnerable women involved in this network were active agents, either as sponsors who consciously decided to be paid for a sham marriage, or were active to recruit these fake brides. In that sense they can be considered as perpetrators. However, some of these women were also victims of the same criminal networks, as they were never paid the share that they were promised.

As far as we can deduct from the narratives, the above examples of Turkish bilateral sham marriages concern commercial agreements between the potential migrant and sponsor. However, bilateral marriages can also be a 'service for friends' where a sponsor enters a relationship just on paper as a favour to the potential migrant so that he or she can obtain a residence permit. We did not identify any explicit examples of such Turkish marriages in our file research, but the Turkish health care provider whom we interviewed did point out that a 'service for friends' can be driven by humanitarian or political reasons among the Turkish community. He remarked that after the coup in Turkey in 1980, sham marriages were a solution for people who were at risk of being arrested for their political activities or ideas: members of certain political organizations with a sister organization in the Netherlands, immigrated to the Netherlands via sham marriages with allies who wanted to help them.

But the respondent also stressed the influence of increasingly restrictive policies and that – as far as he sees this among his networks and patients - people only enter into a sham marriage if it is absolutely necessary, and only for a close family member who is very dear to them now that one has to wait for five years before getting an independent residence permit.

Unilateral Sham Marriages

According to the literature the so-called 'Turkish trick' plays a role in unilateral Turkish sham marriages. A Turkish female migrant with a Dutch nationality who was interviewed illustrates how she came to the Netherlands through such a construction, after her husband's first attempt to get a residence permit through a bilateral sham marriage was unsuccessful.

Turkish-Dutch woman, in her fifties, uneducated

"My husband came to the Netherlands as a 'tourist' in the beginning of the 2000s, to find a job. I stayed behind in Turkey with our very young daughter, and moved in with my parents-in-law. After a while my husband told me that we had to get divorced; he was going to marry an Antillean-Dutch woman and would pay her a good amount of money in order to get a residence permit, and later bring me over there too. He met this woman through a marriage broker; she had already married someone else for money before. After we got divorced, they were married, were living together on paper but not in reality. Meanwhile, she apparently got pregnant from another man. My husband was afraid that once the baby was born he had to acknowledge the baby legally. About a year after the marriage, before he could get a residence permit he divorced this woman. Just before he was to be deported from the Netherlands, he met another Dutch woman at a café. He told her his story, but left out the part that he had a wife and a child in Turkey. This woman apparently pitied him and wanted to help him; this time there was no money involved. For three years they lived together like a real husband and wife. I knew about it, but had no choice. He came to Turkey during the vacations and I got pregnant with our second child. After three years, he got his residence permit, and told this woman that he fell out of love with her. After that, we got married again in Turkey and the children and I came here. I still pity this woman because my husband deceived her; thanks to her my children and I could come here."

This example clearly involves women as active agents and women as victims: a woman who deliberately enters a sham marriage for money while she is in another relationship, the Dutch woman who thought she had entered a real relationship and who is pitied by the Turkish woman for what had happened to her. The Turkish woman, who had to miss her husband for a few years, but earned legal residency for it, can also be considered an indirect victim of this sham marriage. These marriages were imposed on her by her husband, as the ultimate solution. As she was socio-economically dependent on her husband, she had no choice but to accept this migration strategy. In addition, she was left behind with her parents-in-law. After many years she still suffers the psychological consequences of this experience. Charsley and Liversage (2013) describe a similar case in Denmark where the real partner in Turkey felt powerless against the decision of her husband to marry a Danish woman; she was at the same time grateful to her, as she was their 'ticket' to a legal existence and a better life in Denmark. She even wanted to meet her, but her attempts to find the Danish woman failed.

An example from the file analyses shows that not all 'Turkish tricks' turn out to be a 'success', and its gender implications are not always clear. A

Turkish man, in his thirties, who obtained a temporary residence permit as a result of his relationship with a Dutch man, married a Turkish woman in Turkey while he was still in a 'relationship' with his male partner. He applied to the immigration authorities to change his purpose of stay to obtain a residence permit as an entrepreneur. That was rejected. Meanwhile he received a permanent residence permit as a result of his stay with the Dutch partner. Soon after, he applied to bring his wife from Turkey. His first application was rejected because he did not meet the income criterion. During the evaluation of the second application it became clear that he got his permanent residence as a result of a sham relationship – unknown whether this was arranged bilaterally or unilaterally. His residence permit was withdrawn and his wife's application was rejected. It is unknown whether the wife was involved in the construction or continuation of the sham marriage or how she had been affected by it.

Conclusion

This chapter aimed to contribute in filling the knowledge gap regarding the prevalence and manifestation forms of Turkish sham marriages and their gender implications, with a special focus on the Netherlands. European governments invest in measures to combat sham marriages, as they consider such marriages as a form of misuse of admission policies and fraud. Evidence from several studies, including ones from the Netherlands, suggest that there is a gender-bias in the way which immigration authorities deal with marriage-migration applications: applications by female sponsors with migrant men are more often checked than applications by male sponsors with migrant women. According to different authors (e.g. De Hart, 2000, 2001; Wray, 2006; Tamburlini, 2014; Carver, 2016), ideas of women being potentially vulnerable and naïve, prone to deception by migrant men and therefore in need to be safeguarded by nation states lie behind this 'rescue narrative' (cf. Bracke, 2012). In this contribution we focused on the question whether women involved in Turkish sham marriages, regardless of their nationality, are indeed victims of sham marriages.

Results of our study show that an overwhelming majority of Turkish migration marriages in the Netherlands are genuine. However, a small percentage is not. These sham marriages manifest themselves either as bilateral arrangements (where both parties are aware of the purpose of the marriage: a permanent residence for the migrant) or as unilateral ones (where the sponsoring partner is under the impression that the marriage is for love, while the immigrating partner aims at papers).

Figure 4.2 summarizes the manifestations of Turkish sham marriages, encountered in the literature and in the qualitative findings from our file-research and interviews.

Figure 4.2. Manifestation forms of Turkish sham marriages

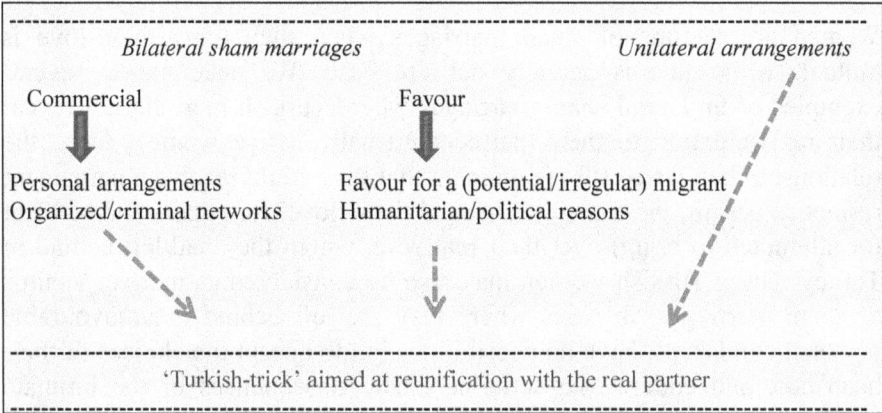

The findings indicate that bilateral Turkish sham marriages can be either commercial or set up as a favour to close family members or political comrades. Narratives of various cases of bilateral, commercial sham marriages show that women involved in these marriages are not necessarily victims, but can be active agents who play an important role in the construction of sham relations. In these cases, women with an EU-nationality act as fake-brides or operate as intermediaries within criminal networks to recruit these brides. In this sense, women take a deliberate responsibility in migration fraud. There is however evidence that some of them come from socio-economically fragile contexts and may feel 'forced' to participate in such marriages: widows, with children and debts. Similar cases were reported in the Czech Republic and Portugal, where single mothers, sometimes with criminal antecedents, acted as sponsors (EMN, 2012), and in Austria where pensioned women in financial crisis, drug addicts and prostitutes were available as fake brides (Digruber and Messinger, 2006). According to a recent study by the Immigrant Council of Ireland (2016), women from EU-countries in the Baltic region with poor education and poor knowledge of English, in extreme poverty and family breakdown took part in sham marriages and were exploited in well-organized networks. A number of them had mental disabilities. In cases where these sponsoring women are exploited, or are not paid their 'fee' by criminals, they can be considered also as victims of sham marriages.

In our research we did not encounter examples of Turkish women acting as sponsors in commercial sham marriages, but it became clear that some are involved in sham marriages in other ways, as active agents. Firstly, by finding a fake groom for money as an ultimate solution to legalize their stay in the host country. Secondly, by operating as active facilitators/ intermediaries in private spheres to find a fake partner as a favour to close relatives or acquaintances who are in need of papers.

Women are victims of sham marriages when they think their love is mutual, while this is actually not the case. We encountered several examples of unilateral sham marriages where Turkish men did not reveal their real intention to their 'partners', usually native women. Once the relationship had lasted till the moment that they could receive a permanent residence permit, these men exchanged their 'love' for papers and brought (or attempted to bring) over their real wife, whom they had left behind in Turkey. These Turkish women may also be considered as indirect victims of sham marriages, in cases where they are left behind in unfavourable personal conditions, have no possibilities but to accept the choices of their husbands, and endure long-term personal consequences of the intimate relations their husbands had in the past.

What do our findings mean for policy and practice in general? Even though only a small part of (Turkish) migration marriages are sham, the simple fact that criminal networks may be involved makes the government checks on sham marriages unavoidable. As the European Commission stresses: it is not only the frequency of sham marriages that matters but also the implication of organised crime (European Commission, 2013/837). Besides, it is unknown what the 'preventive effects' of government controls are. It is also clear that not all woman involved in sham marriages are victims, nor are all victims necessarily female. This raises the question of whether a government policy against sham marriages should not preferably be gender-neutral, directed against any kind of immigration fraud rather than being gender-biased and focussing on victimization of women?

Whether sham marriages will become a more or a less 'popular' strategy among migrants is difficult to foresee, as two conflicting factors are at play. On the one hand, globalization and increased movement of migrants across international borders, and specific to the Turkish case, the recent political developments in Turkey might lead to an increase in marriages for papers. Apart from the possibility of commercial sham marriages, sponsors in Europe with connections in Turkey may be motivated by political and humanitarian reasons to 'service' their fellow citizens, political companions, or relatives. On the other hand, immigration and settlement policies in the EU are becoming increasingly restrictive for non-EU citizens. For example, in 2012, the Dutch government increased the period after which a marriage migrant can obtain an independent residence from three to five years.[20] As a result, one can expect that sham marriages will become less popular among both migrants and sponsors, as the couple has to 'keep up appearances' for a much longer time.

References

Bracke, S. (2012). From 'saving women' to 'saving gays': Rescue narratives and their dis/continuities. *European Journal of Women's Studies*, 19 (2): 237– 252.

Carver, N. (2016). 'For her protection and benefit': The regulation of marriage-related migration to the UK. *Ethnic and Racial Studies*: 1-19.

Charsley, K. and Liversage, A. (2013). Transforming polygamy: Migration, transnationalism and multiple marriages among Muslim minorities. *Global Networks*, 13 (1): 60-78.

Constable, N. (2005). *Cross-border Marriages: Gender and Mobility in Transnational Asia*. N. Constable (ed.). Philadelphia: University of Pennsylvania Press.

Council of the European Union. (2012). *EU Action on Migratory Pressures- A Strategic Response*. 10 May 2012, Brussels.

Engbersen, G., San, M. van and Leerkes, A. (2006). A room with a view: Irregular immigrants in the legal capital of the world. *Ethnography*, 7 (2): 210-242.

Hart, B. de (2000). De goede lobbes en de onbezonnen vrouw. Gemengde relaties en het schijnhuwelijk. *Migrantenstudies*, 16 (4): 246-260.

Hart, B. de (2001). Transnationaal Project Fabienne: Ongelijke behandeling in de rechts-en overheidspraktijk: Oplossingsstrategieën tegen discriminatie naar het voorbeeld van binationale paren: Deelrapport Nederland: Schijnhuwelijken. Nijmegen: Centrum voor Migratierecht, Katholieke Universiteit Nijmegen.

Digruber, D. & Messinger, I. (2006). Marriage of residence in Austria. *European Journal of Migration and Law*, 8: 281-302.

European Commission. (COM/2009/313). Communication from the Commission of the European Parliament and the Council on Guidance for Better Transposition and Application of Directive 2004/38/EC on the Right of Citizens of the Union and Their Family Members to Move and Reside Freely within the Territory of the Member States. Brussels.

European Commission. (2013/837). *Communication from the Commission to the European Parliament, the Council*. The European Economic and Social Committee and the Committee of the Regions. Free movement of EU citizens and their families: five actions to make a difference. COM (2013) 837 final, Brussels.

---

[20] Settlement policy for non-EU migrants who are married or are in a registered partnership with someone from another EU-country than the Netherlands is more generous due to EU-law: they do not have to leave the country if they were living with this partner for at least three years of which at least one year in the Netherlands. But they can get a permanent residence after five years (Aliens Decree 2000/article 8.15/lid 4a; translation from Dutch by the authors).

European Commission. (COM) (2014/284). Handbook on Addressing the Issue of Alleged Marriages of Convenience between EU Citizens and Non-EU Nationals in the Context of EU Law on Free Movement of EU Citizens. SWD (2014) 284 final, 26/9/2014, Brussels.

European Migration Network (EMN). (2012). Misuse of the Right to Family Reunification. Marriages of Convenience and False Declarations of Parenthood. Luxemburg: Publications of the European Union.

Henriksen, M. and Frich M. (2008). Tyrkiske familiesager kulegraves [Turkish family cases are thoroughly investigated], *Berlingske Tidende*, 30 juli 2008.

Huis, M. van and Steenhof, L. (2003). Divorce risks for foreigners in the Netherlands. Paper for Euresco conference 'The second demographic transition in Europe', 19 – 24 June 2003, Spa, Belgium.

Huis, M. van (2007). Partnerkeuze van allochtonen. *Bevolkingtrends*. 4e kwaartal: 25-31.

Immigrant Council of Ireland (2016). *Exploitative Sham Marriages and Human Trafficking in Ireland*. Dublin: Immigrant Council of Ireland.

Kulu-Glasgow, I. Liu, W.Y.J., Jennissen, R.P.W. and Smit, M. (2016). "Deceptive appearances: a study into the prevalence and manifestations of sham relationships in the Netherlands" (in Dutch, with summary in English). In *Cahier 2016-6*. The Hague: WODC. Accessed from http://www.wodc.nl/onderzoeksdatabase/2494-schijnhuwelijken.aspx

Messinger, I. (2013). There is something about marrying…the case of human rights vs. Migration regimes using the example of Austria. *Laws*, 2: 376–391.

Mühleisen, W.; Røthing, Å. and Bang Svendsen, S.H. (2012). Norwegian sexualities: Assimilation and exclusion in Norwegian immigration policy. *Sexualities*, 15 (2): 139-155.

Polish Ministry of Interior (2012): *Misuse of the Right to Family Reunification in Poland: Marriages of Convenience and False Declarations of Parenthood*. Warsaw: Polish Ministry of Interior, Polish National Contact Point to the European Migration Network.

Pöyry. (2010). Marriages of Convenience: A Comparative Study Rules and Practices in Norway, Sweden, Germany, Denmark and the Netherlands. Oslo: Econ Pöyry.

Shevtsova, M. (2013). Acquisition of European Union citizenship through marriage: Citizenship Policies and the Experience of Transnational Couples in Germany and Italy. Budapest: Central European University, Department of Gender Studies.

Staring, R. (2001). Reizen onder regie: Het migratieproces van illegale Turken in Nederland. Amsterdam: Het Spinhuis.

Sterckx, L., Dagevos, J., Huijnk, W. and van Lisdonk, J. (2014). *Huwelijksmigratie in Nederland*. Den Haag: Sociaal en Cultureel Planbureau.

Wolff, van der, A. C. (2012). Misbruik van gezinshereniging: Schijnhuwelijken en valse ouderschapsverklaringen in Nederland. Rijswijk: INDIAC/EMN.

Wray, H. (2006). An ideal husband? Marriages of convenience, moral gate-keeping and immigration to the UK. *European Journal of Migration and Law*, 8: 303–320.

Chapter Five

Undocumented Migrant Women in Turkey: Legislation, Labour and Sexual Exploitation

Emel Coşkun

Introduction

Turkey, a traditionally migrant sending county, has become a destination and transit country for migration and refugee movements since early 1990s. Today, in addition to hundreds of thousands of undocumented migrants, more than 2.7 million Syrians living in Turkey under "temporary protection" status. Previous research suggests that political changes in neighbouring areas, being located at conjunction of the East and West, a closer and cheaper neighbouring country with a relaxed visa regime, and the European Union's (EU) restrictive migration policies made Turkey more attractive for many migrants and tourists (İçduygu and Kirişçi, 2009). Initially, a significant number of transit migrants and asylum seekers, mainly from Afghanistan, Iraq and Iran but also from several African and Asian countries came to Turkey to find their way to enter the wealthy Europe since 1990s. Düvell (2006) points out that the term 'transit migration' refers to several forms of migration such as refugees and labour migrants, regular and 'irregular' migration, and temporary immigration. In fact, while some of these migrants are able to claim asylum since they meet the criteria set by the Geneva Convention, others may stay as undocumented. Therefore it is not easy to differentiate between documented and undocumented migrants especially regarding their participation to labour market during their stay in Turkey. The term 'undocumented' is used specifically for those migrants who have no right to entry, residence or work permit with reference to the restrictive migration policies.

There are also a significant number of migrants from neighbouring countries who primarily came to trade and work in Turkey with tourist visas especially after the break-up of Soviet Union in 1992. Women are the 'pioneers' among this group of migration since the 1990s (Erder and Kaşka, 2003; Yükseker, 2003). Only in 1992, two million 'travellers' entered Turkey from Eastern Europe and former Soviet countries, and many of them were 'petty traders' who sell and buy small-scale of goods with circular movements between the regions (Aktar and Ögelman, 1994: 345). Pioneering women migrants in these circular movements initially crossed Turkey's borders as shuttle traders. The Turkish economy presented good trade opportunities with neighbouring countries and women traders from ex-Soviets had become important trade partners for the wholesalers of Laleli during the early and mid-1990s (Erder, 2011). The 'shuttle trade' (also known as suitcase or petty trade) alone has created an important share of Turkey's foreign trade. In 1996, the size of shuttle trade reached 8.8 billion dollars, which was 10 percent of Turkey's total export (Mustafaoğlu, 1998). This huge economy also resulted in further relaxing the borders between Turkey and the former Soviet countries for the purpose of trade or tourism. People from former Soviet countries (predominantly from Russia, Ukraine, and Moldova) had come to Turkey with 1-3 months long tourist visas as shuttle traders, as employees in families, as domestic workers in farms and in construction companies (Erder and Kaşka 2003; Yükseker, 2003). Turkey has presented a good opportunity to trade and work with its rather a large informal economy. This migration flow has been identified by its circular and gendered nature where women made up the majority as traders or as workers in many sectors where migrant labour exists with the exception of male dominated construction workers (Toksöz and Ünlütürk-Ulutaş 2012).

Major characteristics of this circular type of migration flow are its temporary basis and rare involvement in *illegal* border crossings; however, what makes it undocumented (or *illegal* in the eye of the state officials) is the migrants' involvement in working without documents or staying after the expired visa (Erder and Kaşka, 2003:33). Most migrant women are employed in gendered segments of the labour market informally as domestic workers, sweatshop workers, salespersons in textile stores, waitresses in entertainment places or involved in selling sex (Yükseker, 2003; Gülçür and İlkkaracan, 2002; Erder and Kaşka, 2003; Toksöz et al, 2012). Geographical closeness, relaxed visa regime and the large informal economy together with relatively better economic conditions, demand for cheap labour are considered as major factors that caused this new and gendered circular type of migration in Turkey. Based on a review of the previous research on migration, Toksöz and Ünlütürk-Ulutaş argue that migrants' participation in the labour market "certainly takes different forms in regard to sex" alongside their ethnicity (2012: 86). The scholars argue that migration is also 'feminized' in Turkey similar to many migrant receiving countries where women migrants work is visible in gender specific segmented labour markets (Toksöz and Ünlütürk-Ulutaş, 2012: 107).

Women migrants have been visible especially in high income OECD countries as their proportion is increased from 51 to 52 per cent in the last 15 years (United Nations, 2016). Previous research suggest that the rapid increase of women in waged work without a commensurate change in the traditional division of labour in the home, the gradual disappearance of the welfare state, an ageing society, the marketization of care, and the negative effects of neoliberal capitalist policies on poorer countries have supported the migration of cheap gendered labour, namely women migrants (Shutes and Anderson, 2014; Williams, 2014; Kofman et al. 2000; Ehrenreich and Hochschild, 2002; Sassen, 2001; Lutz, 2010). Tens of millions of women migrate from Third World to First World countries as domestic workers, carers, cheap workers or prostitutes where their services demanded. It can be also argued that the demand for women migrants' labour also make migrant women find jobs more easily in gendered segments of labour markets. Similar to the gendered migration literature, migrant women also became visible both in number and by characteristics of their work in Turkey. Research show that migrant women have been working in some specific sectors such as domestic and care services, garment industry, jewellery or leather production, in seasonal agriculture, or in other service sector jobs such as sales assistants or models, and in prostitution[1] (Gülçür and İlkkaracan 2002; Yükseker 2003; Erder and Kaşka, 2003; Dedeoğlu and Gökmen, 2012; Eder, 2015; Dedeoğlu, 2016; Coşkun, 2016a).

As migrant sending countries have been diversified in the last decades, gendered migration has also been diversified in Turkey both in ethnicities and characteristics. Women from Commonwealth of Independent States (CIS) and African countries have also joined these gendered migration flows and took their position in the labour market. For example, as a result of Turkey's 'African Action Plan' to improve trade to Sub-Saharan African countries, women from remote countries such as Uganda, Kenya, Nigeria, Congo and Senegal also joined in these migration flows (see Heck, 2014;

---

[1] I use the terms "prostitution" and "prostitute" instead of "sex work" and "sex workers". I also use the phrase "prostitution regime" following Outshoorn (2004, 6) to refer to a set of policies and practices surrounding prostitution.

De Clerk, 2013; Coşkun, 2016a). For example Ugandan women come to Turkey as shuttle traders but also as cheap workers in small textile or jewellery ateliers, as domestic workers or as prostitutes (Coşkun, 2016a). Another example could be seasonal migrant workers, Dedeoğlu's (2016) research documents that Georgian women migrants have the majority among migrant labour in tea harvest and hazelnut picking jobs while Syrian women are primary workers in other seasonal agricultural jobs except animal husbandry where Azeri men have the majority.

Although the form of women's migration and ethnicity are diversified in the last decades, their undocumented position remained. As a result of restrictions on migrants, being undocumented shapes women's informal working and living conditions different than men in Turkey. Therefore, based on existing literature and research, this chapter will analyse undocumented migrant women's position in Turkey's migration regime by focusing on legislation on migration, labour market and prostitution regimes. I will argue that current migration and labour regime of Turkey structurally create 'vulnerabilities' for women with a reference to Waite et al. (2015) as they are pushed to work in gendered segments of the labour market informally in most precarious positions. These vulnerabilities do not only facilitate the way for labour exploitation but also result in gendered risks such as sexual harassment or being pushed to sell sex. My aim is to offer an understanding of undocumented migrant women's position in Turkey and the role of the state in the light of migration, labour market regulations and sexual exploitation.

In the next section, I will examine the legal framework of labour and visa regimes, how women's undocumented position takes place and shapes their position in the labour market of Turkey. In the second part, I will describe the gendered risks for women created by the undocumented position, and finally some conclusions and policy recommendations are presented.

Becoming Undocumented: Restrictive Rules on Migrants

In accordance with Turkey's bid for EU membership and to prevent informal working of migrants, there have been important changes in legislations related to citizenship, residence and work permits for 'foreigners'[2] since the early 2000s. The main law on "Work Permits for Foreigners" (No.4817) was put into force in September 2003 and the

---

[2] In all official papers migrants are defined as *foreigners* in Turkey.

Ministry of Labour and Social Security (MoLSS) was authorized to issue all working permits or to restrict them to certain sectors if necessary (ÇSGB, 2016). According to this regulation employers and workers should meet the criteria set by the MoLSS and priority is given to Turkish nationals. According to this regulation the job should be in a sector where there are no restrictions for migrants or there should be no citizen worker who is willing to take the job and the employer should have at least ten citizen workers in a permitted sector. A migrant can access a work permit through an employer prior coming to Turkey or after having a six months resident permit (Ibid). Even if the employer and the employee meet the criteria and provide the necessary documents, the MoLSS might not give the permit as it has the authority to issue work permits. Therefore, the process of applying for a work permit is long and bureaucratic due to the assessment of required documents and involvement of different parties such as Turkish Labour Agency (İŞKUR) and the Migration Management departments. It is also worth noting that employers are expected to pay higher insurance premiums for migrant workers since they are supposed to have high-skills and specific qualifications which cannot be found easily in the local labour market such as knowledge of foreign language and high-tech.

All these difficulties and burden discourage employers, especially when they are not willing to apply for a work permit because of their advantageous position over migrants. In addition to lower wages employers also benefit from most precarious position of migrant workers. As they always fear of being fired or non-payment, migrants become more loyal and reliable hard workers who consent to work longer hours especially in the absence of social rights and due to their lack of choice. Based on her research on post-soviet women migrants in Turkey, Eder (2015:142) also points out the intense vulnerability of new arrivals.

The number of work permits also reflects the unwillingness of employers and the restrictions. The number of work permits was 64,547 and only 16,825 of which were in domestic jobs in 2015 (ÇSGB, 2015: 21-22). Although domestic work is one of the exceptionally 'low-skilled' jobs for which migrant women can get work permits at lesser insurance premiums, the number of permits still remains low compared to the estimated number of hundreds of thousands of women working informally (Toksöz et al., 2012).

Sectorial differentiation of work permits also show the gendered bias of the labour market. Following domestic and care work, the second biggest number of work permits for migrant women is in the hospitality fields. For example women from the Russian Federation and Ukraine account for 60 per cent of tourism sector permits (approx. 5,000 in total) and there is also a growing number of women, mainly from Indonesia (1,900 permits in 2015) and other South Asian countries, who are employed as masseurs at touristic hotel Spa centres (Toksöz et al., 2012:51). These figures also show the sectorial concentration of women migrants with specific ethnicities. Dedeoğlu also points out the gendered bias by showing that while Georgian women can get work permits relatively easy for domestic jobs, they cannot access work permits as seasonal workers (2016). Similarly thousands of migrant women work in different sectors such as textile ateliers, small production ateliers and they cannot get work permits (Coşkun, 2016a). This is also a result of sectorial restrictions on migrants and employer's unwillingness. Overall, these figures also show how Turkey's migration regime is gender biased and discriminates against women as it confines their work options with gendered work such as domestic work, care or hospitality and entertainment sectors.

While the restrictive and bureaucratic employment processes make it difficult to work in the formal labour market, resident permits are also subject to meet the criteria. Law on Foreigners and International Protection (2014:15) requires a safe accommodation or having a guarantor, or a rent contract and other supporting documents such as private health insurance, a bank account with thousands of dollars to obtain a short-term resident permit up to one year. Meeting these requirements is difficult for most migrants who have not enough financial support or social networks. To overcome these difficulties, migrant women used to do circular movements in which they could stay up to three months with tourist visas depending on their nationality but were able to cross the borders and return in a day, so they could continue their stay without waiting for another three months. It can be argued that this visa regime gave rise to circular migration by providing the possibility of staying on tourist visas. However, a new piece of legislation has changed this increase in 2012. Aiming to prevent 'illegal' working and to comply with the EU laws a change was made on tourist visas as of the 2nd February 2012. The Turkish government adopted a new law stating that migrants who come to Turkey with tourist visas cannot stay in Turkey for more than three months and will wait for further three months to re-enter the country. Those who stay with expired visa have to pay a fine at the border and cannot re-enter for a period of time depending on the length of their stay. Without a doubt, this change has a negative effect on migrant women as most of them had and have to violate their visas in order to continue their work as long as they can and become undocumented after one or three months.

The regulations and distribution of limited work permits show that Turkey's migration policy discriminates women and confines them in limited and gendered work options. When the formal employment is considered as a burden and is not desirable for employers, most migrant women consent to work in poor working conditions and stay dependent to their employers when they are undocumented. The majority of migrant women (and men) work informally in most insecure labour conditions under Turkey's migration regime. As Waite et al. argue all these factors contribute the structural production of vulnerability of migrants who find themselves in "commonplace exploitation" as a result of interaction of "broader political, economic, social and gendered processes" (2015: 3). While migrant women's work choices are constrained by restrictive migration and labour regulations they are considered as cheap, easily controllable and exploitable labour in Turkey. In fact, most migrants cannot defend their rights against employers because of their undocumented position and with the fear of deportation. Being undocumented, however, has also different meanings and risks for women as they are also susceptible to gendered violence.

Sexual Exploitation of Migrant Women

The restricted migration and labour regulations cause most migrant women to become undocumented and to work in the low-skilled and low waged positions in the labour market. Previous research show that migrant women's working conditions both in domestic and public spheres usually are poorer than local workers. Although there are exceptions, they usually work in less qualified and gendered positions that citizen workers are not willing to take. These low-waged and low-skilled positions usually require limited mobility such as sitting or standing long hours, flexible and over working, isolated work environment and involve in assisting other workers such as cleaning the final products (Coşkun, 2016). Therefore not just employers but also local workers get benefit by hiring migrant workers to low-skilled positions. Sometimes the amount of wage, the length of work and their lower positions also reflect this discrimination as most migrants do the dirty works. Even in the same work, migrant can have hierarchy as the newcomers or different ethnicities have the lower positions such as sub-Saharan African women migrants (Ibid). They usually suffer from the risk of non-payment, high dependence on employers, mediators or agencies, language barrier, lack of information about rights, mistreatment of employers, discrimination, racism, emotional, physical and economic violence, unhealthy food and accommodation (Toksöz et al. 2012; Coşkun, 2016a; Yalçın, 2015; Erder and Kaşka, 2003).

Women's position in the labour market as undocumented migrants with no rights and limited work options make them dependent on employers who consents to poor working conditions especially when they are considered as 'illegal workers' with the fear of deportation. While migrants take the jobs at the bottom of the labour market they are also considered as harder workers, more loyal and reliable due to their limited job options and knowledge of their rights. In fact, there is a demand for women migrants not just for their labour as domestic workers but also as cheap workers in different sectors and as prostitutes. My previous research shows that the reason behind the demand for migrant women labour is not just related to their 'hardworking' nature but also related to sexual expectations of employers (Coşkun, 2016a). This sexual demand is especially visible in some small and middle scale textile factories and production ateliers in the area where most employers have 'foreign lovers' (Ibid). Sexual harassment of employers is even reflected in the media coverage as 'private rape rooms' of employers (Patronun özel tecavüz odası, 2014). In fact, asking for sex from migrant women in exchange for paying the deserved wage is a common practice among employers against Ugandan women (Coşkun, 2016a).

In the absence of labour rights and as a result of informal working, employers' sexual harassment has become commonplace. With the fear of being deported, most women not only consent to lower wage, poor working conditions and extreme labour exploitation but also remain silent in case of sexual harassment. In fact, previous research show that migrant women face the risk of sexual harassment wherever they work (Toksöz and Ünlütürk-Ulutaş, 2012; Kalfa, 2008, 2012; Coşkun, 2016a; Biehl, 2014). Most undocumented migrant women cannot defend their rights and in case of sexual harassment they usually keep quiet or quit their jobs with leaving their wages behind (Coşkun, 2016a). Even if a migrant woman complains about sexual harassment, her undocumented and migrant position usually takes priority and even may result in deportation. This situation of non-punishment for gendered violence and involuntary silence of women is well known by most employers that further encourages sexual harassment and abuse of undocumented migrant women. The stigmatisation of migrant women as 'prostitutes' and the prostitution regime of Turkey also create further vulnerabilities as it will be discussed in the next section.

Being undocumented not only affect migrant women at workplaces but also in their social life as it creates 'unequal social relations' between migrants and citizens as Anderson (2013) argue. Previous research also shows that landlords, local shop owners or even ordinary citizens can take advantage of migrant women's undocumented position. For example, during our research in 2011 (Toksöz et al. 2012), we found out that migrant women were being stopped by fake police officer in order to get some money from a migrant woman in the absence of a work permit or a valid visa. Taking advantage of migrants' position is especially visible in some districts where different migrant groups live. For example a recent study also shows how landlords in Kumkapı look for 'bayan' (female) migrant tenants to rent their rooms with a romantic or rather sexual request (Biehl, 2014:12). While most undocumented migrants cannot have any work or rent contracts and therefore cannot claim any rights in case of any conflict with the landlord, many migrant women eventually find themselves vulnerable to sexual requests of their landlords or other male tenants (Ibid). Therefore, in addition to being known as hard workers and cheap labour, migrant women are also perceived as easily controllable and even sexually exploitable tenants.

Without a doubt, there is a demand for migrant women as low-skilled workers in gendered segments of the labour market, as tenants but also as 'lovers' and prostitutes. This demand is also backed by the prostitution regime in addition to the migration and labour regimes of Turkey.

The Demand for Migrant Women in the Sex Industry

There is a high demand for migrant women in entertainment and commercial sex in Turkey. Although commoditisation of women's bodies and the expansion of the sex industry globally can be considered as a general reason for boosting the sex industry in Turkey, it is well known that the breakup of the Soviet regime and inflow of women migrants has helped to increase demand as it diversifies the sexual service industry (Çokar and Yılmaz-Kayar, 2011:51; Toksöz and Ünlütürk-Ulutaş, 2012). Prostitution is a legal occupation in Turkey, however, migrant women are not allowed to work as prostitutes by the legislation on citizenship and the Passport Law. The law No.5682 forbids prostitutes to enter Turkey by Article. 8: "Prostitutes and the persons who incite women to prostitution and the persons who make white women trading and any types of smugglers" (The Passport Law, 1950). Therefore migrant women who sell sex are classified as 'illegal' prostitutes and as criminal offenders not based on the nature of the act but based on citizenship even if they have valid visa. In addition, if a migrant woman is arrested on the suspicion of prostitution, she is a subject to compulsory medical examination for sexually transmitted diseases (STDs) and according to the result she can be deported. Migrant women are subject to deportation based on working 'illegally' in prostitution and/or for having STDs even if they have a valid visa. Therefore if a migrant woman is accused for prostitution there is a high risk of deportation especially in the absence of any visa (Coşkun, 2016b). In summary, there is a high possibility of deportation for migrant women considering the high stigmatisation of migrant women as 'prostitutes' and the burden of proof usually lies with the woman in cases of prostitution accusations in Turkey (Ibid).

Previous research emphasises the strong stigma and perception of 'Natasha the prostitute' ('voluntary') towards migrant women from the former Soviet republic and this perception is also supported by the media (Erder and Kaşka, 2003). Gülçür and İlkkaracan pointed out that harassment against the blond 'Natashas' 'not only come from local men on the streets but also from the police, who have been known to arbitrarily harass, detain, ask for bribes, and/or deport any blonde, foreign-looking woman, regardless of her visa status and regardless of whether she is a sex worker or not' (2002:414). Most recently, my research also show the high stigmatisation towards sub-Saharan African women as voluntary prostitutes or sexually exploitable women (Coşkun, 2016a). Ayata *et al.* (2008: 61) argue that the representation of migrant women in the media as equal to 'voluntary' prostitutes has helped in stereotyping migrant women and made invisible the demand side of prostitution and trafficking for sexual exploitation. Questioning the demand side, Ayata *et al.* (2008: 59) point to a biological reductionist approach where male sexuality and the sexual needs of men are naturalised and seen as a necessity among society. The common perception of migrant women's voluntary involvement in prostitution combines with the toleration for paying for 'illegal' prostitution. In fact, although there is a zero tolerance to street prostitution, men who are involve in street prostitution cases are usually free to go after a report is taken by the police while most migrant women are under the risk of deportation.

Research show how migrant women's involvement in prostitution strongly pronounced that most migrant women are perceived as prostitutes and encountered sexual harassment wherever they work (Ege, 2002; Kalfa, 2008; Biehl, 2014; Coşkun, 2016a;). This stigmatisation does not only create a high demand for the sexual services of migrant women but also pushes women into prostitution and makes them vulnerable to exposure to sex trafficking (Coşkun, 2016a).

Conclusion

There is no room for doubt that the role of the state in migrant women's position in Turkey is important considering all the facts above. Limited job opportunities together with bureaucratic and restrictive employment processes for migrants, no resident permit options and unwillingness of employers make it difficult for migrants to work formally in Turkey. Turkey's migration regime discriminates migrant women by driving them into undocumented and insecure positions. The labour market also confines them into gendered segments of the labour market as domestic workers, sweatshop workers or as prostitutes. In fact, in private or public spheres, migrant women do less waged, dirty and unwanted gendered jobs left from citizen women workers. No possibility of staying and working legally except limited number of gendered jobs (domestic work) and with no punishment for violation of rights basically encourage different forms of gendered violence against migrant women. In fact, in case of violation of human rights or sexual harassment, a migrant woman's undocumented position usually takes priory and prevents her from seeking justice, and even may result in her deportation. This fact is well known by employers and that's why also hiring a migrant woman becomes attractive for employers. Previous research shows that sexual harassment becomes a commonplace for undocumented migrant women.

Unfortunately, Turkey's migration and labour regimes creates structural vulnerabilities for migrant women. Therefore the government should take preventive measures against exploitation of undocumented migrant women and migrants in general. These preventive measures could be done by including migrants in policy making from a humanitarian and gendered perspective. Previous research suggests that a legal protection such as residence permits empowers migrant women in their relations to other parties and protects them to a certain level. Therefore policy making should include facilitating to access resident and work permits. Criminalising this gendered violence against migrant women with a zero tolerance is also a must. In addition, there is an urgent need for a civil and multilingual crisis centre where undocumented migrant women can seek help without fear of deportation when they face gendered violence and sexual harassment. Migrant women should be also given the opportunity to stay and work in Turkey on a humanitarian base as survivors of gendered based violence. This can be referred to Article 4 of "Council of Europe

Convention on preventing and combating violence against women and domestic violence" also known as Istanbul Convention (Council of Europe, 2011). Turkey has signed most international conventions against the violence against women including CEDAW and Istanbul Convention. The convention recommends protection of any women in case of gendered violence without discrimination on any ground (Ibid). It means it also include migrant women regardless of their undocumented status. Protective mechanisms also should be put in force with free health, accommodation and legal support to migrant women.

Unless there is a gender sensitive and human centred approach backed up by viable options for undocumented migrant women, any efforts will be insufficient to prevent women (or men) migrants from being exploited and sexually harassed. What is good for undocumented migrant women is also good for other migrant groups and the state is responsible to protect migrants from gendered violence and being exploited in order to build gender equality and a fair society.

References

Aktar, C. and Ögelman, N. (1994). Recent developments in east-west migration: Turkey and the petty traders. *International Migration,* 32 (2): 343–354.

Anderson, B. (2013). *Us and Them.* Oxford: Oxford University Press.

Anderson, B. and Shutes, I. (2014). "Migration and care labour: theory, policy and politics". In *Migration, Diasporas and Citizenship.* B. Anderson and I. Shutes (eds.). Houndmills, Basingstoke, Hampshire: Palgrave Macmillan.

Ayata, A. et al. (2008). Türkiye'de İnsan Ticaretinin Farklı Formlarına Olan Talebin İncelenmesi. Ankara: Uluslararası Göç Örgütü.

Biehl, K. S. (2014). Exploring Migration, Diversification and Urban Transformation in Contemporary Istanbul: The case of Kumkapı. MMG Working Paper 14-11. Göttingen: Max Planck Institute for the Study of Religious and Ethnic Diversity.

Castles, S. and Miller, M. J. (2009). *The Age of Migration: International Population Movements in the Modern World. 4th edition.* Basingstoke and New York: Palgrave Macmillan and Guilford.

ÇSGB (Çalışma ve Sosyal Güvenlik Bakanlığı). (2015). *Yabancıların Çalışma İzinleri. 2015 Yılı Raporu.* [Online] Accessed from http://www.csgb.gov.tr/media/3209/yabanciizin2015.pdf

ÇSGB (Çalışma ve Sosyal Güvenlik Bakanlığı). (2016). Yabancıların Çalışma İzinleri Hakkında Kanun (No. 4817). *Mevzuat Online* Accessed from http://www.mevzuat.gov.tr/Metin.Aspx?MevzuatKod=1.5.4817&MevzuatIliski=0&sourceXmlSearch=

Çokar, M. and Yılmaz-Kayar, H. (2011). *Seks İşçileri ve Yasalar: Tükiye'de Yasaların Seks İşçilerine Etkileri ve Öneriler.* Istanbul: Human Resource Development Foundation.

Coşkun, E. (2016a). Türkiye'nin göç rejiminde toplumsal cinsiyet faktörü: Ugandalı göçmen kadınlar örneği. Fe Dergi: Feminist Eleştiri, 8 (1): 91-104.

Undocumented Migrant Women

Coskun, E. (2016b). Consent' issue in sex trafficking and evidences from Turkey. *Social Politics,* 23 (3): 437-458.

Council of Europe (2011). *Council of Europe Convention on Preventing and Combating Violence against Women and Domestic Violence.* Council of Europe Treaty Series - No. 210 (online) http://www.coe.int/en/web/conventions/full-list/-/conventions/rms/090000168008482e

De Clerk, H. M. (2013). Sub-Saharan African migrants In Turkey: A case study on Senegalese migrants in Istanbul. *SBF Journal,* 68 (1): 39-58.

Dedeoğlu, S. and Gökmen, Ç. E. (2011). *Göç ve Sosyal Dışlanma: Türkiye'de Yabancı Göçmen Kadınlar.* Istanbul: Efil Publishing.

Dedeoğlu, S. (2016). Türkiye'de Mevsimlik Tarımsal Üretimde Yabancı Göçmen İşçiler Mevcut Durum Raporu: Yoksulluk Nöbetinden Yoksulların Rekabetine. Ankara: Kalkınma Atölyesi.

Düvell, F. (2006). Crossing the fringes of Europe: Transit migration in the EU's neighbourhood. [Online]. *Centre on Migration, Policy and Society Working Paper No. 33.* University of Oxford. Accessed from: http://www.compas.ox.ac.uk/publications/ working-papers/wp-06-33 on 4 February 2013.

Eder, M. (2015). "Turkey's neoliberal transformation and changing migration regime: The case of female migrant workers". In *International Human Mobility: Key Issues and Challenges to Social Theory.* S. Castles (ed.). pp. 133-150.

Ehrenreich, B. and Hochschild, A. R. (2002). *Global Woman: Nannies, Maids and Sex Workers in the New Economy.* London: Granta Books.

Erder, S. (2011). "Zor Ziyaret: Nataşa mı? Döviz getiren bavul mu? Eski Doğu Bloku ülkelerinden gelen kadınların emek piyasasına girişi". In *Birkaç Arpa Boyu: 21.Yüzyıla Girerken Türkiye'de Feminist Çalışmalar, Prof.Dr.Nermin Abadan Unat'a Ağmağan.* S. Sancar (ed.). İstanbul: Koç University, pp. 191-219.

Erder, S. and Kaşka, S. (2003) Irregular Migration and Trafficking in Women: The Case of Turkey. Istanbul: IOM.

Gülçür, L. and İlkkaracan, P. (2002). The "Natasha" experience: Migrant sex workers from the former Soviet Union and Eastern Europe in Turkey. *Women's Studies International Forum,* 25 (4): 411–421.

Heck, G. (2014). Transit göçten ticarete: Türkiye'deki Kongolu göçmenlerin yaşam koşulları ve gündelik stratejileri. *Toplum ve Bilim,* 131: 68-83.

İçduygu, A. and Kirişçi, K. (2009). *Land of Diverse Migrations: Challenges of Emigration and Immigration in Turkey.* İstanbul: İstanbul Bilgi University.

ILO (International Labour Organization) (2005). *Labour Migration Policy and Management –Training Modules.* International Labour Office, Bangkok.

Kalfa, A. (2008). Ex-Eastern European Countries Origin Trafficking and Women Working in the Sex Sector. Ankara: Ankara University. Master's Thesis.

Kaşka, S. (2009). "The new international migration and migrant women in Turkey: The case of Moldovan domestic workers. In *Land of Diverse Migrations: Challenges of Emigration and Immigration in Turkey.* A. İçduygu (ed.). Istanbul: Istanbul Bilgi University, pp.725-804.

Keough, L. (2008). Driven" Women: Gendered Moral Economies of Women's Migrant Labor in Postsocialist Europe's Peripheries. Doktora Tezi. Amherst: The University of Massachusetts.

Kofman, E., Phizacklea, A., Parvati, R. and Sales, R. (2000). *Gender and International Migration in Europe*. London: Routledge.

Law on Foreigners and International Protection (2014). Republic Of Turkey Ministry Of Interior, *Directorate General Of Migration Management Publications* [Online] Accessed from http://www.goc.gov.tr/files/files/YUKK_I%CC%87NGI%CC%87LI%CC%87ZCE_BASKI(1)(1).pdf

Lutz, H. (2010). Gender in the migratory process. *Journal of Ethnic and Migration Studies* 36, (10): 1647-1663.

Morokvasic, M. (1983). "Women in migration: beyond the reductionist outlook". In *One Way Ticket. A.* Phizacklea (ed.). London: Routledge, pp.13-33.

Morokvasic, M. (1991). Fortress Europe and migrant women. *Feminist Review,* 39: 69-84.

Mustafaoğlu, Z. (1998). *Rusya Krizinin Turkiye Ekonomisi Uzerine Etkileri*. Devlet Planlama Teşkilatı. http://ekutup.dpt.gov.tr/dunya/rusya.pdf Accessed: 6/10/2011.

The Passport Law. (1950). *Law Number: 5682 of 15 July 1950*. [Online]. http://www.legislationline.org/documents/action/popup/id/8984 Accessed: 8/7/2014.

Patronun Özel Tecavüz Odası. (2014). *Cumhuriyet Gazetesi*, 13 July 2014. Accessed from http://www.cumhuriyet.com.tr/haber/turkiye/93675/Patronun_ozel_tecavuz_odasi.html

Toksöz, G. and Ünlütürk-Ulutaş, Ç. (2012). Is Migration Feminized? A Gender- and Ethnicity-Based Review of the Literature on Irregular Migration to Turkey.

Toksöz, G., Erdoğdu, S. and Kaşka, S. (2012). *Türkiye'ye Düzensiz Emek Göçü ve Göçmenlerin İşgücü Piyasasındaki Durumları*. IOM Türkiye.

United Nations. (2016). *International Migration Report 2015: Highlights*. New York: United Nations. http://www.un.org/en/development/ desa/population /migration/ publications/migrationreport/docs/MigrationReport2015_Highlights.pdf

Waite, L., Craig, G., Lewis, H. and Skrivankova, K. (2015). "Introduction". In *Vulnerability and exploitation at work: Precarious migrant lives*. L. Waite, G. Craig, H. Lewis and K. Skrivankova (eds.). London: Palgrave Macmillian.

Williams, F. (2014). "Making connections across the transnational economy of care. In *Migration and Care Labour: Theory, Policy and Politics*. B. Anderson and I. Shutes (eds.). London: Palgrave Macmillan.

Yalçın, Ç. (2015). Türkiye'de ev hizmetlerinde çalışan göçmen kadınlar ve ekonomik şiddet. *Fe Dergi*: 50-60.

Yükseker, D. (2003). Laleli-Moskova Mekiği: Kayıtdışı Ticaret ve Cinsiyet İlişkileri. İstanbul: İletişim Yayınları.

Zlotnik, H. (2003). *Global Dimensions of Women Migration*. Migration Policy Institute. Vol.10 Accessed from http://www.migrationinformation.com/ Feature/display.cfm?id=109 on 11 January 2010.

Chapter Six

Family Perspective in Migration:
A Qualitative Analysis on Turkish Families in Italy

Gül İnce Beqo

Introduction

The main purpose of this research is to understand the migration phenomenon from a family perspective because family, as a relational social unit, can be a lens which reflects the transnational and intergenerational impacts of migration both on receiving and sending society. For the main purposes of this study I will refer to a relational definition of the family. Donati (2007) argues that family, different theoretical sociological approaches have framed/ considered the family as a structure of roles created by external factors like the social division of labour, the level of economic development, the type of political regime or communicative technologies. This vision caused the exclusion of the relational character of the family from its definition. Family is thus seen as a unit which is driven by the external forces that are not directly related to human experience "while it should be observed instead as a morphogenetic network of relations, or rather as a primordial and original network emerging from the mediations that the family, as a *sui generis* social relation, act between nature and culture, between public and private, between individual and society (Donati, 2007: 10). It is situated in 'between' two categories like public and private or like individual and society because it is a sphere of different societal functions and whatever happens within it influences even the other forms of social relations. (Donati, 2012). So, the transfigurations occurred in the family sphere have its impacts also on the territorial community which surrounds the family since "family is a relational good[1] for all" (Donati, 2012: 40). The social subjectivity of the family stems from it being a communitarian relationship based on a full reciprocity between gender and generations. But there is even more: the family is a social subject since it is "a subject of relational contracts and rights, a sphere of societal functions, a holder of its own citizenship (Donati, 2000), and a *sui generis* link between liberty and responsibility" (Donati, 2007: 139). These components refer to family's symbolic character; in fact, the family is not constituted only by a material or legal entity, the long-term committed relations among who establish it, is the main condition of being family.

Migration through the lens of the family

If family is a 'communitarian relationship' (Donati, 2012), how the relational aspect of family can be a useful lens to understand the migration phenomenon? This is the question which it will be tried to explain in this section.

Zanfrini (2008) argues that in the last decades the sociology of migration focused only on the incorporation process of migrants in the receiving country. In other words, within the theoretical debate the social dynamics of sending country were nearly always neglected. Migration was considered a unidirectional movement while migrants were -male-individuals and social character of migrants was not an important variable to understand such phenomenon. What are the motivations of such vision? Why are migrants such a long time considered as merely individuals but not as a member of their families or of larger communities? Different scholars tried to understand the reason of this reduced vision of migration which see migrants as simple individuals. The main reason why our understanding of the roles of the family in migration process is still in its infancy (Zlotnik, 1995) is the heavily economic emphasis on migration studies (Kofman, 2007). For long the neoclassical economics theory, which considers migration either as a result of the international labour demand or as a rational choice of individuals to maximize individual income, was the

---

[1] The term 'relational good' was introduced into the theoretical debate by different authors from different disciplines in the second half of the 1980s. The sociologist Pierpaolo Donati introduced the term 'relational good' within the relational perspective to define a kind of common good which can't be reduced neither to individual goods nor to the sum of individual goods (Donati, 2007). Relational goods are based on the practice of reciprocity and can be enjoyed only through the social relation. They emerge from the orientation of actors producing or consuming together a common good which can't be produced or consumed outside that reciprocal relationship" (Donati, 2007, Donati and Solci, 2011).

dominant theoretical model to explain migration (De Haas, 2008). So, because of this economic and individual emphasis, the family migration studies have always been marginalized theoretically, methodologically and empirically (Kofman, 2007). Zlotnik (1995) argues also that family activities that can't be measurable in monetary terms are not taken into consideration because of the tendency to view work in terms of activities that can produce income. This consideration caused not only the exclusion of family activities from migration studies but also the exclusion of women. The latter will be considered in depth in the next section.

Starting from the 80s the above-mentioned exclusions become relevant to many scholars and different perspectives were developed to answer them. The family perspective (Boyd, 1989; Fawcett, 1989; Faist, 1997; Gurak and Caces, 1992; Scabini and Rossi, 2008) considers family as the main decision-making unit and migrants as family members with specific roles and responsibilities (as wife/husband, mother/father or as children of migrants). This perspective argues that family has a considerable influence on the migration decision-making mechanism as well as the adaptation (or non-adaptation) process of the migrants into the receiving society. Gozzoli and Regalia (2005) explain with three main motivations why assuming a family perspective is important for migration analysis. First, as it is shown in the figure below, family migration is the main component of international migration flows (OECD, 2014).

Figure 6.3. Permanent immigration in OECD countries by category, 2007-2012

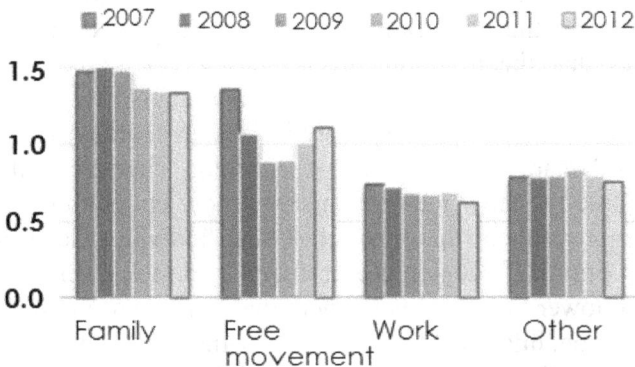

Source: OECD International Migration Database (http://www.oecd.org/berlin/Is-migration-really-increasing.pdf)

Second, through family perspective, not only the initial phase of migration, but all stages can be analysed since family strategies orient both migration decision and the adaptation process in the receiving country. Moreover, a relational family perspective allows also take into consideration what happens in the country of origin with those family members left behind (elder parents, children, and spouse). It may also influence those left behind by shaping the representations they have about the receiving society: this usually produces what is called a "culture of migration", that is when migration is "deeply ingrained into the repertoire of people's behaviour, and values associated with migration become part of the community's values" (Massey et al. 1998: 47). Lastly, this approach helps to understand the long-term effects of migration both for the receiving and sending country in an intergenerational perspective by taking into consideration all members of the family which are -directly or indirectly-subjected the migration experience. Boyd (1989) argues that such perspective is also able to illustrate migration outcomes like non-migration, immigration, return migration or the perpetuation of migration flows since the personal networks, in this perspective, are considered not only as a social and financial assistance, but also a source of information.

Another reason why family perspective is a useful lens to understand the migration dynamics is because the neoclassical economic migration theories try to understand the motivations of international migration but they do not focus on the reasons of why people don't migrate although the push factors which drive them to leave their home. Boyd (1989) argues that household's survival mechanisms can help to comprehend the reason why migration does not always occur. Timmerman and Hemmerechts's (2015) research confirms and supports Boyd's assumption. In their field research based on the data gathered in the EUMAGINE project[2], they (2015) argues that the migration decision, both to migrate and to not migrate, is highly affected from the transnational family ties. The research includes two provinces of Afyon, a city in Western Turkey; the district of Emirdağ and Dinar. The first one is a region characterized by high emigration while the latter has comparatively low emigration. One of the most significant result of this research is that, individual level migration aspirations in Emirdağ, a region characterized by a high level of 'culture of migration' are lower than in Dinar, where that 'culture of migration' lacks. So, the socio-economic conditions, especially the recent financial crisis of Europe are more familiar for people who live in a migration-impacted region thanks to their relations with the Turkish immigrant communities in

---

[2] For more information please see: http://www.eumagine.org/default.aspx

Europe and it strongly affects their migration decisions (Timmerman & Hemmerechts, 2015).

The Role of the Family in the Pre-Migration Phase: The Migration Decision

The decision to migrate may seem at first sight to be in the hands of the individual mover but it is a decision that takes place in reference to strengths and weaknesses of her or his household[3] and there are three main determinants in migration decision: age, marital status and gender roles within the family context (Cohen and Sirkeci, 2011).

Kanaiaupuni (2000) argues that the likelihood of migration decreases with age for both genders and especially in a young age (20-29) men are more likely to migrate than women. Nevertheless, the probability to migrate is higher for women than men after the age of 50. This is because in many cases women migrate for family reunification or once their children are grown-up they join their husbands abroad.

In generally, the migration decision of young people is determined by their parents depending on rules, social regulations and expectations. In some cases, the migration decision involves all the members of the family – even if some researches confirm that the larger becomes the family the lower the likelihood of moving from one place to another (White, Moreno and Guo, 1995) – and sometimes it may involve only the children like in the case of Filipinos "who will go into debt to send their children to training programs at national universities, where they can master new skills as nurses and caregivers. Parents assume their children will take their newfound skills, gain employment in the U.S., and support their families in the Philippines once they have established themselves in North America (Kingma, 2005; Parreñas, 2005, as cited in Cohen and Sirkeci, 2011).

Marital status is another variable which determines the migration decision. Kanaiaupuni (2000) finds that marital status causes different migration propensities for women and men. While for men it is not a significant determinant it becomes an important one for women since unmarried women are more likely to migrate then married ones. For Cohen and

---

[3] For Cohen and Sirkeci (2011) a household is definitely more than a place within which a family lives. They (2011) argue that a household is created by and in reference to the people who live in it. They are fluid (since they may refer to different family unit forms) and finite units (since they have a beginning and an end in specific places). What characterizes a household is also its symbolic and ideological purposes and it is a unit within which cultural and social norms and beliefs are produces, reproduced and changed.

Sirkeci (2011) the reason why marital status has different effect on women and men is because "married women often face a series of traditional beliefs that are barriers to mobility and suggest their migration as problematic at best and extremely dangerous at worse. In transnational migration, they are likely to follow the trajectories of their spouses, brother or fathers and often with a certain time lag. Their resource also go to family but where men can have an adventure women are at risk" (Cohen and Sirkeci, 2011: 24-25).

Another variable which determines the migration decision is gender since "men and women encounter different barriers to decision making at home as well as abroad" (Cohen and Sirkeci, 2011: 26). Hoang (2011) finds that Vietnamese women's decision about their own migration was in part constrained since they were forced to negotiate for their own interests in order to preserve the family harmony. The restrictions on women's migration is partly due to traditions of sending society but also "the result of restrictions imposed by receiving countries. While Arab countries, for instance, remain a major destination for female movers from Southeast Asia (a group that is mainly employed as domestic workers), Turkish migration to Arab countries was almost completely male-dominated and focused on construction (Icduygu and Sirkeci 1998, as cited in Cohen and Sirkeci, 2011: 26).

The Role of the Family in the Post-Migration Phase: The Settlement

Once migration has occurred, norms about the meaning of migration and maintenance of attitudes toward familial obligations over time and space is transmitted by families (Boyd, 1989). In the after-migration stage family is subjected to a bilateral interaction; the bond with the origins[4] and that with the host society (Scabini and Rossi, 2008). On one hand, it tries to maintain the loyalty to the existing cultural norms and values and family members left behind, on the other hand, it reorganizes its own dynamics according to the host society's social norms by renegotiating the roles, expectations and values among the family members. "In settlement transitions the family retains its central functions throughout the process of adaptation to the modes of settlement. It is grounded in the particular needs of its members" (Valtonen, 2008: 123). Different needs provide different settlement processes. Wulff and Dharmalingam (2008) in their research on

---

[4] It's a characteristic concept of the relational-symbolic model (Scabini and Cigoli, 2000) which focuses on the relational and symbolic dimensions of family ties in an intergenerational perspective.

the role of social connectedness find that, for immigrant families, to be parent is an important variable that determines their neighbourhood activities; i.e. parents, compared to non-parents, are more likely to become involved in neighbourhood activities. They (2008) demonstrate that the families with children show much stronger social connectedness (72 % more) than families without children.

It is told also before; family, in the settlement phase, tries to remain loyal to the existing culture. Baskin (2015) examines the loyalty to the mother tongue to preserve the ethnic culture in the migration context and she finds that Turkish women living in France, through their use of language especially in the family context, are perceived as bearers of culture and tradition. Some researches demonstrate that women may perceived as the main protector of the tradition while others argue that women, due to their multiple role within the family allow them to deal with alternative source of fulfilment, are better able to cope with barriers to successful integration and they also may positively shape the family's settlement experience by ensuring that their children are successfully integrated. (European Commission, 2008).

Research Methodology

In terms of methods, the investigation is qualitative and exploratory in nature and focuses on the Turkish communities in Italy, which are mostly under-studied. "A qualitative method is considered appropriate for an analysis of concepts and themes derived from an exploration of social funds, *about which relatively little was known and about which in-depth understanding was desired.* (Bowen, 2005, p.210, *italics are mine*). In exploratory research, as Lincoln and Guba (1985) suggest, social phenomena are investigated with minimal a priori expectations in order to develop explanations of these phenomena. Thirty-two semi-structured interviews were conducted with sixteen couples of Turkish migrants (interviews were conducted with both spouses but -as long as possible- separately) in Novara, a province in the Piedmont region. Several difficulties were encountered in the fieldwork. First, the difficulty to obtain access to the research field. What helped gain access to the participants was my experience as a volunteer in different schools as teacher of Italian for children of Turkish immigrants. In the beginning, I was able to make contact with Turkish families not as a researcher but as a teacher for their children. Finally, one of the mothers agreed to introduce me to other families.

The first interviews were conducted in the spring of 2015 but after late July 2015, when Turkey and the PKK broke out the peace negotiations, gaining access to the field became harder than before. Nobody wanted to talk despite my insistence that we would not talk politics but their migration decision. Some interviews were conducted without a recording machine at their request. One of the interviewees, after our interview called me many times to ask me not to report everything they had said.

Lastly, since I experienced beforehand that conducting the interviews in pairs reduces the freedom of expression of women, I decided to interview husbands and wives separately. Therefore, the other main challenge was to convince men about this since they often disagreed on the fact that I could interview their wives alone.

Turkish Migration in Italy

In Italian there are many common sayings about Turks; as like "mamma li turchi!" (oh my God, the Turks!), "prendere il turco per i baffi" (to grab the Turk's moustache) or "fumare come un turco" (to smoke as a Turk), etc. However, it seems that these common says do not make reference to current Turkish presence in Italian territory since according to a survey done by Institute for Research on Population and Social Policies in 2002 about Italian attitudes and opinions towards foreign immigrants (Bonifazi, 2006) only 0.5 % of 3000 participants responds "Turks" when they are asked which nationality do they think about when it comes to immigrants.

The Turkish immigration is a recent phenomenon for Italy; in fact, the first significant immigration from Turkey to Italy start in the late 90's and they were mainly Kurdish asylum seekers as indicated by Armelloni (2008);

> "(...) The first ship arrived 2nd of November in 1997 in Santa Maria di Leuca carrying 550 Turks / Kurds; 19th of November arrived another boat in Calabria carrying 374 citizens of the same nationality; then on December 27 other 837 asylum seekers reached in Calabria Badolato with the ship called Ararat and still 386 Kurds were received in the first days of January 1998."

Turkish migration into Italy may be categorized as a "chain migration" (Grieco 1987a: 51); i.e. a process where "migrants who have been successful in obtaining employment transfer resources and information on employment opportunities back to their families in their area of origin (...)" According to data published by Istat (2015) (The Italian National Institute of Statistics) in 1st of January 2015 there are, with no clear count of illegal immigrants, 19.782 Turkish residents in Italy and most of them live in the northern area of the country as indicated in the table below:

Table 6.1. Classification of Italian regions sorted by number of Turkish residents (January 2015)

	Male	Female	Total
Lombardia	3.945	3.395	7.340
Emilia-Romagna	2.087	1.634	3.721
Piemonte	1.117	762	1.879
Liguria	938	721	1.659

Source: Italian National Institute of Statistics (ISTAT, 2015)

According to the data above (provided by Istat) nearly equal numbers of males and females show that the rate of family reunification is relatively high. The main sending regions of immigrants are Central Anatolia Region (Sivas, Konya), Mediterranean Region (Kahramanmaras-Pazarcik), Southeastern Anatolia Region (Gaziantep). In northern Italy, there are different cultural and religious organization like as DITIB Italy (Turkish-Islamic Union for Religious Affairs), Milli Gorus Italya Teskilati (Italian Organization of the National Vision), Italya Alevi Bektasi Kultur Birligi (Italian Bektashi Cultural Organization).

Results

Family Networks and Migration Decision

The literature offers different researches on the relationship between family networks and migration decision (Boyd, 1989; Palloni et. al., 2001; De Jong, 2010). Jeager (2000) in his research where he examines the locational tendencies of legal immigrants to the U.S., finds that family networks tend to attract migrants to the same geographic areas. This is even the case of Turkish migrants in Italy since the interviews demonstrate that family network is one of the most important element to decide where to migrate. In some cases, it becomes even the only significant reason to migrate:

> *"(...) If there weren't my brothers I wouldn't come...No, I wouldn't come to Europe, I wouldn't even think about it. Because in Turkey I was comfortable. I had a job. I mean, we had a good economic situation. I was in Antep, my father was working and me too. I have 8 brothers. 8 brothers... What could happen to us?"*

Most of the people that have been interviewed come from Pazarcık, a town in the southern part of Kahramanmaraş Province, situated in the

Mediterranean Region. The homogeneity of the population does not depend only on sampling technique that is used to reach the population (snowball sample) but also on the fact that Italy is an important destination for this community. (Gurbuz, et al., 2003). It is a typical example of male migration where men migrate first and later occurs the family reunification. Italy is nearly always the last option to migrate for Turkish migrants. They first try to go to other European countries like Germany, Switzerland or France where they can count on welfare states and if they can't obtain asylum in these countries then they come to Italy. Another reason why they choose to come to Italy is because, according to them, they aren't sent back from Italy to their country of origin, although their illegal status:

> *"Anyone here went back {to Turkey} like this from Italy. If he goes, he goes for his choice. I never heart someone who is sent back to Turkey. No, no, never! No one left Italy like this. In fact, for this they come to Italy."*

Migration, Family Relationship and Gender Roles

The interviewed women came to Italy to follow their husband and many of them are legal immigrants since they arrived for the family reunification. They are all families where traditional gender roles of male breadwinner and female caretaker dominate. All the women who are interviewed lived with the extended family of husband during his absence. Since, among those interviewed there is a high presence of consanguineous marriage (especially between first-cousins) during this period it is experienced even the transformation of their different family roles; it can be defined as a period of transition from aunt to mother in-law, from uncle to father in-law and from nephew to daughter in-law. The interviewed women often told to not have a significant decision-making power in this period. It is indicated also from Abadan-Unat (1977) that non-migrated women have a major autonomy during the absence of their husband especially if they live in a nuclear family context. So, is it possible to argue that to live with husband's extended family may obstacle the possibility to gain an autonomous decision-making capacity during the absence of husband? Abadan-Unat (1977) argues also that in extended families, another family member may have considerable influence on left-behind women in the absence of the migrant husband. It may be a reasonable argument even according to the interviewed women's experience since some women don't want to go back in Turkey even for holidays because when they go to

Turkey they spend more time with their parent-in-law than with their parents, and not all have a good relationship with in-laws. One of the most fundamental problems is the changes in the way their husband behaves toward them in the presence of his relatives:

> *"(...) Here they call him (her husband) a henpecked. Why? Because he always asks my opinion before doing something. In Turkey? No, he wouldn't be like this. Here, he is alone and he needs me... Here we are alone. He needs me, he asks everything to me..."*

> *"(...) When we go to Turkey he changes ... He sees his parents and forgets me. He doesn't want even to touch me..."*

Returning to Turkey

Waldorf (1995), in her research on the determinants of international return migration intentions of guest workers in Germany (1970-89), hypothesizes that return migration intentions are determined by personal attributes, residential and job satisfaction and three time-dependent variables: a temporal trend, a duration effect, and years prior to retirement. In this research, I argue that the intensions of return migration are influenced and mostly determined by gender norms and roles; i.e. men and women have different expectations and motivations about (not) returning to their place of birth.

When it is asked their first impressions of Italy (and of Europe, in generally) they respond that it was not always very positive. Europe did not, and even now doesn't correspond at all to that of their imagination;

> *"...No, it wasn't what I expected... It was worse! I... Sometimes when we look the TV we think, they show Europe, they show always beautiful place of Europe. They never show place like this neighborhood. They show seaside... I thought a place furnished with lights... A beautiful place... I thought a more beautiful place. When I saw first I thought, but it's like my village! It's like Turkey."*

So, all the participants told that in the beginning they had many difficult times because they suffer extreme homesickness but despite that, at the moment, the women, seem to be more willing than men to continue to live in Italy.

> *"In the beginning, it was difficult but now I got used, I am comfortable here..."*

> *"If my husband says to go back we go, of course, but I can live in here, too."*

Mainly, there seems to be two reasons which convince the women to remain in Italy; first one is the freedom to do things which can't be easily done in their hometown;

> *"You know what? Even only to drive this bicycle would be enough for me to live in Italy all my life"*

> *"...For my family, wouldn't be a problem... No... I don't think so but for that of my husband the fact that I learn to drive would be a big problem. In here I don't care, I love driving..."*

While the second reason why they would like to continue to live in Italy is the possible transformation of the relationship with their husband;

> *"Here we are more united; he has only me in here. If I go in Turkey, he doesn't ask me anything..."*

> *"(...) If we were in our country... If we were in our country {our} marriage would be more difficult. Do you know why? When we are there {in Turkey} we have the parents of my husband, there are my parents, our brothers... We sacrifice our time to stay with our parents. (...) In our hometown if a man shares his ideas with his wife, they say that you ask your wife's permission (...). In here it is different. We dedicate all our time to each other"*

Men very often expressed their desire to go back to Turkey and when they don't want to do, it's usually because of their negative perception about return migrant or economic concerns rather than the family-related reasons;

> *"If I would like to remain in Italy I bought a house here... No! No! All my investments I make in Turkey, all the money I earn I send to Turkey. (...) Earlier I go back, better is..."*

> *"If I would have half than what I have in here I would be ok in Turkey... Doesn't matter how many friends you have in here, in Turkey even the air is different..."*

> *"I don't have anything. How can I go back to my town?"*

> *"Once you come to Europe you can't go back anymore in Turkey. They ask you; what did you earn all these years?"*

On the other hand, when men are asked about their relationship with their wives, the words like 'transformation' or 'change' have nearly always a negative connotation.

> *"(...) If you know yourself you don't change. If you want, you can go to America. But you should know yourself. But if you lose yourself... For example, {she says} 'I cook and you wash the dishes' or 'I wash the dishes and you cook'. Those are the people who lost themselves... But if you have the respect for your husband..."*

> *"(...) For Turkish men, they have the priority. I speak even for myself. I don't ask neither to my wife for something. It doesn't change neither in Turkey nor in abroad... Nothing changes... Everything is same... In our house, it is like this..."*

> *"(...) If people know themselves they don't lose their way of being. We, Turkish men, are the part of a patriarchal system. I mean, honestly, I don't believe in gender equality. (...) If you don't lose your tradition everything becomes a bed of roses. (...) If you lose your identity, and I should underline that the European lifestyle is very favourable for this, everything becomes senseless".*

Conclusion

There are different researches about the impacts of migration, especially men's labour migration, on family relationships and gender roles. Many of them demonstrate a positive relationship between men's migration and non-migrating women's autonomy and decision-making (Sarker and Islam, 2014; Yabiku et al., 2010; Hadi, 2001). On the other hand, Abadan-Unat (1977) argues that migration as a component of modernization has a double-faced impact on women's emancipation. On one hand, it promotes emancipation while on the other hand it creates a "false climate of liberation, which actually does not surpass increased purchasing power, thus resulting only in pseudo-emancipation" (Abadan-Unat, 1997: 55).

In this research, I analysed the relationship between the migration experience and the transformation of family practices among migrating family members and anyway, in some cases, it is found a positive relationship between the interviewed women's autonomy/decision-making and their migration experience. What emerges from the interviews is that, in some cases, the migration process transforms the women's family relationships in their favour, even if it occurs in a very limited way. Away from family ties (especially from those of their husband) they feel freer to manage their family relationships and their lives. Such transformation determines also the return migration intentions. A large number of women expressed their desire to not go return to their place of birth because their migration experience in Italy seems to give them, even if it is sometimes only in domestic sphere, an area of freedom and more possibility to be taken into account by husband. May the fact that this occurs only in the domestic sphere depend on the migration duration? Since it is a quite short-term migration experience for the Turkish immigrants in Italy, would be further changes (for better or for worse) related to women's decision-making power and autonomy over time? For now, we don't have the answers of these questions; yet to answer them, through a comparative or longitudinal field study, can significantly contribute to the improvement of this research. On the other hand, as it argued also by Bever (2002) the changes in gender relations brought about by migration are understood better by studying also non-migrant families' negotiation of gender roles in the household; so, to extend the research on Turkey, where non-migrant families can be studied, may also improve the results of this research.

References

Abadan-Unat, N. (1977). Implications of migration on emancipation and pseudo-emancipation of Turkish women. *International Migration Review*.11 (1): 31–51.

Armelloni, M. (2008). Comunità e ambiguità: il caso dei rifugiati kurdi, in Van Aken Mauro (2008) *Rifugio Milano. Vie di fuga e vita quotidiana dei richiedenti asilo*, Napoli, Carta Editore, pp. 163-179.

Baskin, J. F. (2015). "Turkish women in Alsace: Language maintenance and shift in negotiating integration". In: I. Sirkeci, B. D. Şeker and A. Çağlar (eds.). *Turkish Migration, Identity and Integration*. London: Transnational Press London.

Bever, S. W. (2002). "Migration and the transformation of gender roles and hierarchies in Yucatan" In *Internal and Transnational Migration: Case Studies from Mexico and the U.S.* (SUMMER, 2002), Urban Anthropology and Studies of Cultural Systems and World Economic Development, 31 (2), pp. 199-230.

Bonifazi, C., (2006). Le opinioni degli Italiani sull'immigrazione straniera, Quaderni, Consiglio Nazionale delle Ricerche, Istituto di Ricerche sula popolazione e le politiche sociali.

Boyd, M. (1989). Family and personal networks in international migration: Recent developments and new agendas. *International Migration Review*, 23 (3): 638-670.

Bowen, G. (2005). *Preparing a Qualitative Research-Based Dissertation: Lessons Learned*. The Qualitative Report. Volume 10, Number 2 June 2005 208-222.

Cohen, J. H. and Sirkeci, I. (2011). *Cultures of Migration. The Global Nature of Contemporary Mobility*. Austin: University of Texas Press.

De Haas, H. (2008). *Migration and Development: A Theoretical Perspective*. International Migration Institute, James Martin 21st Century School, University of

Oxford, working papers n. 9. Accessed from: https://www.imi.ox. ac.uk/pdfs/wp/wp-09-08.pdf

De Jong, G. F. (2010). Expectations, gender and norms in migration decision making. *Population Studies, A Journal of Demography,* 54 (3).

Donati, P. (2000). "The new citizenship of the family: concepts and strategies for a new social policy". In *The New Citizenship of the Family. Comparative Perspectives,* H. Cavanna (ed.). Ashgate: Aldershot, pp. 146-173.

Donati, P. (2007). Old and new family policies. The perspective of relational sociology. *Sociologia, Problemas e Praticas,* 54: 127-159.

Donati, P. and Solci, R. (2011). I beni relazionali. Che cosa sono e quali effetti producono, Bollati Boringhieri, Torino.

Donati, P. (2012). *Family Policy: A Relational Approach.* FrancoAngeli Edizioni, 1a edizione, Milano, Italy.

European Comission. (2008). Interface: Immigrants and National Integration Strategies: Developing a Trans-European Framework for Analyzing Cultural and Employment Related Immigration. Accessed from http://www.ulb.ac.be/ socio/germe/documentsenligne/interface.pdf

Faist, T. (1997). "The crucial meso-level". In *International Migration, Immobility and Development.* T. Hammar, G. Brochmann, K. Tamas and T. Faist (eds.). Oxford: Berg, pp. 187–217.

Fawcett, J.T. (1989). Networks, linkages, and migration systems, *The International Migration Review,* 23 (3), Special Silver Anniversary Issue: International Migration an Assessment for the 90's: 671-680.

Gozzoli, C. and Regalia, C. (2005). *Migrazione e Famiglie,* Il Mulino, Bologna.

Grieco, M. (1987a). Keeping it in the Family: Social Networks and Employment Chance, Tavistock Publications.

Gurak, D.T. and Caces, F. (1992). "Migration networks and the shaping of migration systems". In *International Migration Systems. A Global Approach.* M. M. Kritz, L.L. Lim and H. Zlotnik (eds.). Oxford: Clarendon, pp. 150-176.

Gürbüz, M., Karabulut, M. and Sandal E. K. (2003). An examination of illegal immigration from Turkey to Western Countries: A Case Study of Pazarcık (Kahramanmaraş), *Marmara Cografya Dergisi.*

Hadi, A. (2001). International migration and the change of women's position among the left-behind in rural Bangladesh. *International Journal of Population Geography,* 7 (1): 53- 61.

Hoang, A. L. (2011). Gender identity and agency in migration decision-making: Evidence from Vietnam. *Journal of Ethnic and Migration Studies,* 37 (9).

Istat. (2015). *Stranieri Residenti al 1° gennaio – Cittadinanza.* http://dati. istat. it/ Index.aspx?DataSetCode=DCIS_POPSTRCIT1 Accessed: 10 November 2016.

Istat. (2015). *Resident Foreigners by Age and Sex on 1st January 2015 Italy.* http://demo.istat.it/strasa2015/index_e.html Accessed: 21 November 2016

Jaeger, D.A. (2000). *Local Labor Markets, Admission Categories, and Immigrant Location Choice.* Hunter College and Graduate School CUNY Working Paper. http://conference.iza.org/conference_files/amm_2004/ jaeger_d138.pdf

Kanaiaupuni, S. M. (2000). Reframing the migration question: An analysis of men, women, and gender in Mexico. *Social Forces,* 78 (4): 1311-1347.

Kofman, E. (2007). Family-related migration: a critial review of European Studies, *Journal of Ethnic and Migration Studies,* 30 (2).

Lincoln, Y. S. and Guba, E. G. (1985). *Naturalistic Inquiry.* CA: Beverly Hills: Sage (as cited in Bowen, 2005).

Massey, D. S., Arango, J., Hugo, G., Kouaouchi, A., Pellegrino, A. and Taylor, J. E. (1998). *Worlds in Motion. Understanding International Migration at the end of the Millennium.* Oxford: Clarendon Press.

OECD (2014) *Is Migration Really Increasing? Migration Policy Debates,* Accessed from http://www.oecd.org/berlin/Is-migration-really-increasing.pdf

Palloni, A., Massey, D. S., Ceballos, M., Espinosa, K. and Spittel, M. (2001). Social capital and international migration: A test using information on family networks. *American Journal of Sociology,* 106 (5): 1262-1298.

Sarker, M. and Islam, S. (2014). Husbands' international labour migration and the change of wives' position among the left-behind in rural Bangladesh, ISSN (Paper) 2224-5766 ISSN (Online) 2225-0484 (Online), 4 (16).

Scabini, E. and Cigoli, V. (2000). *Il Famigliare. Legami, Simboli e Transizioni* [Family identity: Ties, Symbols, and Transitions]. Milan: Raffaello Cortina.

Scabini, E. and Rossi, G. (2008). *La migrazione come evento familiare, Studi Interdisciplinari sulla Famiglia* n. 23. E. Scabini and G. Rossi (eds.). Milano: Vita&Pensiero.

Timmerman, C. and Hemmerechts, K. (2015). "The relevance of a 'culture of migration' and gender dynamics in understanding migration aspirations in contemporary Turkey". In N Abadan-Unat and G. Mirdal (eds.). *Emancipation in Exile Perspectives on the Empowerment of Migrant Women.* İstanbul: Istanbul Bilgi University Press.

Gurak, D.T. and Caces, F. (1992). Migration Networks and the Shaping of Migration Systems. International Migration Systems. A global Approach. Oxford: Clarendon.

Yabiku, S., Agadjanian, V., and Sevoyan, A. (2010). Husbands' labour migration and wives' autonomy. *Popul Stud* (Camb), 64 (3): 293–306.

Valtonen, K. (2008). Social work and migration: Immigrant and refugee settlement and integration. *Contemporary Social Work Studies,* Ashgate Publishing.

Waldorf, B. (1995). Determinants of international return migration intentions. *The Professional Geographer,* 47 (2).

White, M. L., Moreno, L. and Guo, S. (1995). The interrelation of fertility and geographic mobility in Peru: a hazards model analysis. *International Migration Review* 29 (2): 492–514.

Wulff, M. and Dharmalingam, A. (2008). Retaining skilled migrants in regional Australia: The role of social connectedness. *International Migration and Integration* 9: 147-160.

Zanfrini, L. (2008). "Dai "lavoratori ospiti"alle famiglie transnazionali". In *La Migrazione Come Evento Familiare.* E. Scabini and G. Rossi (eds.). Milano: Vita e Pensiero.

Zlotnik, H. (1995). Migration and the family. *Asian and Pacific Migration Journal,* 4, (2-3).

Chapter Seven

Marriage and Divorce in the Context of Gender and Social Capital: The Case of Turkish Migrants in Germany

Sevim Atila Demir and **Pınar Yazgan**

Introduction

The immigration phenomenon has been recently analysed as a complex process in the context of globalisation and dynamism (e.g. Cohen and Sirkeci: 2011; Sirkeci, 2009; Yazgan, 2016). There are various hypotheses which have been employed to explain the immigration phenomenon, which describes mobility from one location to another. It is observed that these immigration hypotheses have become pluralistic and socio-cultural in nature as opposed to individualistic and economy-centred and that the individual's choice has come to the forefront. The choice here is a preference made by individuals to increase their income. Immigration is based on a cost-benefit analysis, and it is assumed that it occurs voluntarily and with the free will of the immigrant, based on their own economic concerns. In this new economic hypothesis, it is claimed that massive social units rather than individuals decide to immigrate, not to increase their incomes, but to decrease or mitigate their risks. This hypothesis widens both the subject and purpose of immigration and portrays the immigration decision not as an individual act of the immigrant, but as the common decision of social units or institutions. In this framework, immigration is mainly read as the decision of a family or household and it follows in this context that immigration would also be "the immigration of social networks". The immigration network hypothesis emphasises that the presence of relatives, acquaintances, friends or just countrymen in the immigration location decreases the costs and risks of immigration. As for the institution hypothesis, this can be explained as the institutionalisation of large-scale immigration and the more systematic working of the network hypothesis. Social capital is important for the network and institution hypotheses because their role in immigration is valid, not only for the beginning but also for the progression of the immigration (Massey et al., 1993; Chiswick, 1999; Sirkeci, 2003; Sunata, 2014: 87).

However, the relationships established after immigration do not always have the capacity to support this decision. Women constituted 44% of the interprovincial immigration between the years of 1995 and 2000 in Turkey. When their reasons to emigrate are examined, migration depended on one of the family members relocating and immigration was related to searching for and finding employment. Marriage immigration is defined as reunion with a spouse during or after the marriage in a different location and is a somewhat neglected topic due to its gender specific nature. When examined, it would appear that the individual who relocates through marriage immigration is usually the woman and she might be ignored due to being passive and dependent during the immigration process. Women represent a higher percentage of related immigration or immigration through marriage. Percentage of female immigrants who emigrated as the result of the relocation of a family member or through marriage is 52.6%. Thus it is seen that more than half of women participate in immigration without being directly dependent on push and pull factors. According to the national immigration balance sheet, the population which participated in interprovincial marriage immigration between the year of 1995 and 2000 was 355,712 and this number corresponds to 7.4 % of all the immigration that took place. If the marriage number of 500-550 thousand in the early 2000's in Turkey is considered, it might be estimated that approximately 13-14% of these marriages ends up with immigration and 94% of the individuals who participate in the immigration through marriage phenomenon consist of women (Ozgur and Aydın, 2010: 21; Ozgur and Aydın, 2011: 31).

When external migration is in question, women's participation occurred in certain stages. Sending workers to foreign countries and the immigration process to Germany in particular stemmed from the idea that it would be useful for the development of society, industrialisation, and westernization. A further motivation was the severe economic conditions which Turkey was facing in the 1960s. In the first period, married men came to Germany by leaving their wives and children behind (1960-1963). The labour department established "guest worker" employment bureaus and started this process by employing specialised personnel from Germany. At the beginning, no serious efforts were made to address the problems of foreign workers, thinking that they would return after working in Germany for a specific period of time. In the second period, the pace of immigration increased when immigrant men took their wives and children with them and workers who had spent a period of at least two working years in Germany started to bring their families with them (1963-1965). In the following period (1966-1973), employers and labour exchange agencies gave priority to women workers. Thus immigration reached its climax with migrations starting with female workers followed by their husbands (Sirkeci et al., 2012; Atila Demir, 2010). The termination of immigrant worker employment in 1973 caused the problem of making the immigrant worker population permanent and this situation improved the possibility of family reunification, marriage migration and employment for female workers. "Guest worker" employment was officially terminated with the development of the oil crisis on November 23, 1973. The people who sought to relocate to Germany through family reunification were obliged to have the financial means to support the lives of relatives who stayed in Germany. One in every seven branch workers was an immigrant worker in that period in Germany. This migration meant the transfer of human labour to rich countries (Berger and Mohr, 1976: 69). We can classify the labour force sent to Germany from Turkey as an initial movement of the migration in years between 1961 and 1968, with the summit years between 1969 and 1973, the decadence years between 1974 and 1976 and finally the recuperation and mobilisation years after 1976 within this framework.

The gathering of individuals migrating from Turkey specifically in certain locations caused a ghetto-like lifestyle. Social differentiation, behavioural disorders and social disconnections occurred as a result of this (Turan, 1992: 89-93). The fact that 50% of the families with Turkish origin reside in only 4% of the German lands exemplifies this situation (Kastoryano, 2000: 105-106).

Social networks are accepted as a critical level of analysis in mobility and immigration research, as they involve information about particular characteristics of the actors. These networks provide information regarding the analysis of the relationships of the individual, his/her friends and even their friends' habits and their level of happiness (Faist, 2003). For example, according to Framingham Heart Research conducted on 1,020 interrelated individuals in 2000, the happiness and sadness levels of individuals are affected by the network they belong to (Christakis-Fowler, 2009: 9/192). Social relationship networks are being focused on especially to define long-term human behaviours. Trust and support lie heavily inside the relationship networks concept. This concept is usually used with the same meaning as social support and loyalty (Kadushin, 2012: 70-71).

We benefit from social relationship networks in many fields during our daily lives. These networks cause better definition of our daily routine interactions. The power of networks came into being with the social capital concept in social sciences. This phenomenon reveals the efficiency and multidimensional structure of the social networks (see e.g. Coleman, 1988; Putnam, 1995; Bourdieu, 1986). These networks bring social capital to life.

Social Capital and Marriage

Social capital is the sum of having relationship networks which consist of mutual institutionalised relationships and sources which provide support and reference to their own members. Social capital provides the strength that keeps the society together. That is why social capital includes the norms which enable individuals to act together in a more formal definition. This trust-based definition enables us to better focus on the sources of social capital (Bourdieu, 1986: 61; Pieterse, 2003:7; Woolcock and Narayan, 2000: 3).

The main theme of social capital is that communication networks are a major wealth. This wealth is defined by the trust in family, neighbours, colleagues, government, police, etc. (Field, 2006:16; Narayan and Cassidy, 2001: 67). Tocqueville mentions the political functions of social capital in democracies and states that modern democracies have gone through the way of establishing volunteering institutions due to supporting extreme individualism in his book "Democracy in America" (Fukuyama, 2001: 11). Social capital brings a spirit of unification, and it fundamentally belongs to society itself. Unlike other types of capital, social capital is intrinsic to the relationships between actors. According to Coleman, when individuals do something for each other, this causes an expectation of the performer and obligation for the performed. The main emotion here is trust (Coleman, 1988: 102).

Thus, the form of social capital which encompasses obligations and expectations in social life is observed more frequently. Putnam has summarised the elements of social capital as trust, norms and obligations based on reciprocity and relationship networks. Honesty, friendship, social relationships between individuals and families are the funds of social capital. Providing the social needs through these funds is the essential point (1995:65-67; Woolcock and Narayan, 2000: 5). In daily life, these social relationships are established through marriage. The relationships between family and relatives with their friends and acquaintances are expected to be frequently repetitive and long-term. They are seen as a foundation for the creation of social capital, involving relatively closer and more similar relationships. Putnam defines relationship networks with this form as Bonding Social Capital and these networks might slightly involve obligations in the relationships. The same social capital is frequently observed in workplaces when choosing employees, to minimise risk. Thus, determinism and the application of control over behaviours manifest over time in the marriages brought about by bonding social capital networks.

One of the downsides of social capital is that it might decrease or limit the tendency of group members to cooperate with people outside the group (Field, 2006: 45/126). According to Urry, locational things cannot be separated from social ones. Different locational individuals (1999: 97) bring cultural adoption and differentiation together with locational differentiation, especially after immigration. Even though various social relationships can be initiated and maintained by kinship and affinity, it is not enough. Friendship demands similarity (Gans, 1961: 135). According to the Network Hypothesis, a network of immigrant relationships is among the elements which incentivise migration. As mentioned earlier, these networks are the social capital on which they can apply to get help and find jobs. The migration policies supporting family reunion reinforce the immigrant relationship networks and popularise them (Massey et al., 1993; Yazgan, 2010: 34). In particular, the social relationships and norms in the stated immigrant country gain more significance than the homeland. The Turkish case in Germany is an example in point of how a temporarily defined labour force transforms into a neighbourhood and communal formation in the country to which it is emigrating (Castles and Miller, 2008: 292/ 306). People who have immigrant acquaintances and immigrant associations are more likely to migrate. And their social capital expectancy is higher during the first migration period (Massey and Aysa, 2005: 5). This situation is much more effective in the marriage process.

The fact that immigrants with Turkish origins have formed a lifestyle together different from the dominant culture has also influenced marriage and family structures. Marriage migrations can be evaluated within this concept. Marriages display an increased frequency in the second generation, it was observed that first and second generations encouraged their children to marry someone from Turkey to sustain and maintain their cultures and reinforce their bonds with Turkey.

It is seen that marriage migrations are an extension of human labour migrations when the German example is taken as a basis. When the reasons for migrations are inspected according to their levels of density, they can be classified as: college education (1,398), employment (1,256), language learning and education apart from college (103), other (83) and humanitarian reasons (81) (Migrationsbericht, 2006: 111). German born people are not included in these statistics. When men's and women's migrations are inspected, both in Turkish migrations and in foreign migrations, the percentage of female migration through marriage is higher. It is equally important that marriage immigration will affect the status of a woman in this sense, as women get more responsibility through marriage migration. According to the statistics, the density of international kinship relationships and the most obvious example of this fact reveals itself as international marriages.

More than half the second generation population chose spouses from Turkey. That is why most international marriages resulted in migration to Germany (Strassburger, 2004: 6-9). More than 61% of the Turkish people who became German citizens and married in German Registry Offices brought their spouses from Turkey (Strassburger, 2004: 215). When the determinant factors of international marriages are considered, it is seen that demographic factors, social and cultural sources and individual preferences play significant roles (Sirkeci, 2009; Cohen and Sirkeci, 2011).

Not being able to adapt to the regional structures and life standards in the marriages brought about by migration can result in experiencing this limitation in a severe manner. Even though the networks which immigrants have strengthen their social capital, they bring a social control network along with them due to the transfer of homeland-based relationships to the host country (Yazgan, 2010: 234). The social relationship networks of immigrants with their own society are stronger in order to protect their own social elements in the country to which they migrated. Marriage migrations can also be evaluated in this context. Especially when we consider the fact that imported marriages increased in frequency in the second generation, it is observed that first and second generations have encouraged their children to marry someone from Turkey which they saw as the way to sustain and maintain their own cultures and reinforce their bonds with Turkey (Atila Demir, 2011: 910). Marriage migration ranks second after the most common form of external migration, which is human labour migration. According to 2006 data, Turks have migrated to Germany mostly for marriage or domestic reasons (10,195) (Atila Demir, 2010: 73). The individual who migrates through marriage does not have the same opportunities as the one who migrates with a group or family. Although the individual has similar language and cultural lifestyle with the migrated family, he/she would have to adjust to them to a greater level (User, 1996: 558).

Marrying a spouse from Turkey is defined as the result of the desire of immigrant families to keep in touch with Turkey and maintain their values, such as staying connected to their culture. This is also a way to continue migration. As a consequence, some problems (loneliness, being dependent on spouses, language problems, etc.) come along with the marriages through migration. The husbands of these women want to keep them dependent in every way. Thus, a woman learning the host language or making friends puts the established system at risk. That is why there are some deterrent measures in these families to prevent the imported bride from leaving (Kaya and Kentel, 2005: 151-153). As a result, after the migration marriage, bonding social capital networks change over time, affecting the likelihood of divorce.

Divorces in marriages which occurred through traditional bonds - since all the bonds come along with the migration - take place as a result of the transformation of these bonds into means of oppression. The locations where women migrated through marriage have low social control over the external group. However, they have higher control over the internal group because marriage has occurred through social networks. This contradiction affects the awareness level of women and causes transformation in the social gender patterns. This study approaches the immigration, social capital and divorce relationship within the context of social gender.

Data and Method

The field study, which involves a survey of the reasons for getting divorced of 161 divorced couples with Turkish origins in Germany in 2010, constitutes the first phase of the study. The fundamental reasons for divorce and their patterns have been discovered as a result of this study. The major reason for divorce is determined as the socio-cultural difference between the spouses. The second most important reason is determined as the intervention of the families in the marriage and its effect on the marriage. 72 of the 111 female participants who joined the survey described coming to Germany through marriage. 62 of the participants who joined the survey stated that they had arranged marriages, and the remaining 42 said they married out of love (Atila Demir, 2010: 150). According to the results of this survey, interviews were devised with certain categories and the individuals fitting those categories were interviewed.

We have collected detailed information on eight individuals from Germany, who married through social networks and subsequently got divorced. All eight of these people are women. The influence of social networks in the transformation of gender has been formed as goal-oriented for the sampling of female participants. In the previous study, the number of women was twice the number of men (see Atila Demir, 2010). Seven of the interviewees were second generation immigrants. One individual can be defined as 3rd generation. Seven of the interviewees came to Germany through marriage. The other one was born in Germany. All of the participants married through social networks based on trust.

The interviews with eight divorced individuals were inspected in two dimensions. The first was the effect of social networks and social capital before marriage and the second was the effect of social networks and social capital during and after divorce. This part was analysed within the framework of the "countryman", "oppression/limitation", "social relationships", "family oppression", "kinship relationships" phenomena. The transforming effects of these relationship conditions, which were stated at the beginning, were focused upon. In these two processes, the change in the manner of the effect of social capital was approached. Whether the marriage has occurred through migration or not is social networks have a bonding dimension.

Interviews were conducted with semi-structured survey forms and personal points of view, and explanation forms shared by the participants about the subject have been investigated thoroughly (Akmehmet Şekerler, 2015: 186). A voice recorder was used in the interviews to transcribe all of the records. Interviews were used as the qualitative research method and descriptive research design data as the approach. These are aimed to be periodic as a process, descriptive regarding observations, descriptive in the light of data, and exploratory concerning findings.

Within the context of determined concepts and beyond the thematic analysis, statements of the participants regarding social gender were also analysed. Discourse analysis is a resolution based on the context. Social reality is re-established through discourse. Through the contexts - social relationships, family effect, cultural difference, kinship, social gender roles - used by the interviewees to explain certain situations in their statements, it was possible to analyse how they established reality. By what words does the speaking individual state what she wishes to state? What kind of connection has been made in the stated elements?

Analysis is performed by focusing on these questions (Akar and Martı, 2015: 249). Discourse maintains its existence on social levels and societies gain their way of thinking by establishing the connections between symbols and meanings from their discourse. Discourse is a complex social practice. The discourse which comes into existence through language is an entire system with various functions (Celik and Eksi, 2008: 100-101). For this reason, each individual's realities are examined with the effect and structure of social capital through face-to-face interviews and micro level analyses in this study.

The primary research questions of this study are:

- What is the extent of the relationship between marriage migration and social relationship networks?

- Does the negative form of social capital affect the marriage structure set up in the migrated country through social capital tools?

- What kind of effect do social networks have on social gender?

All of the interviewees are individuals who married based on a feeling of trust. Trust and cultural affinity are essentially the first notable elements in the marriages of immigrant societies. Five out of the eight interviewees met their ex-husbands through relatives and the other three through friends. This is to say that the marriages took place through social networks based on trust relationships.

Analysis and Discussion: Marriage, Divorce and Social Capital in the Context of Migration

When we analyse the social capital context, it is observed that the positive and good aspects and effects of this context were most focused on. Ultimately, social networks are defined as a value. Besides this, the downsides of social networks received attention. In particular, Bourdieu underlines the inequality caused by social capital. According to the results of the study conducted in the USA, education level and financial status affect the foundations which these individuals are subscribed to, their numbers and thus the trust level. The same situation is valid between the races and a condition might exist where social capital encourages inequalities between the races. Social capital is seen as the property of privileged groups and, in addition to that, the right to use the advantages of social capital is distributed unevenly. Social networks appear as the primary target of social capital studies. Even though they have a positive meaning, they involve some negative context in some situations. In a nutshell, social capital emphasises that social networks are valuable.

Networks might be intertwined inside the social system. Social capital has two main results, social capital investments and individual social capital. Individual social capital might conduct social capital investments. Bourdieu defines social capital as the potential power obtained within the family and the social environment (Bourdieu, 1986; Kadushin, 2012: 162; Field, 2006: 107-111). Hence, this power contains certain risks as in all kinds of power. The most typical and bonding is the situation where the feeling of trust intertwines with the feelings of obligation and fear. Having a bond or being a member of a group might also involve group consciousness and thus negative sanctions towards people outside the group at the same time. In this sense, social capital might also be used to create negative feelings. Putnam (1995) also considered the negative results of social capital, even though he emphasised that the positive aspects had more weight. Even Coleman accepted that social capital might have bad results and exemplified this by showing that when people cooperate for their own benefit, this might damage others. The thing that needs to be emphasised in this context is the negative effect of social capital on the demands and behaviour of humans. The solidarity of the group might discourage individuals to the point where they decide to break away from the group. This situation causes group rules to oppress personal preferences and demands, keeping group members in a state of dependence at all times. In some cases, these networks may force family members to comply with group rules, explaining the influence of family members on their preferences.

This bonding effect essentially feeds on the fear of the possible consequences of negative social capital. This situation reveals itself clearly in the influence of parents on children's choice of spouse (Putnam, 1995; Field, 2006: 104-125; Coleman, 1988). This influence is more dominant in immigrant families because social capital is related to a cultural bond and unity at the same time. Immigrant societies focus more on cultural ties as a result of the strains of immigration. This causes the social capital to be more productive, both in a positive and a negative sense. The clearest manner of this is observed in marriages which occur through families. When arranged marriages from one country to another are used as immigration strategies, the status balance between families breaks down, and contradictions in relationships might occur (Akpınar, 2007: 146). This situation might make the dark side of social capital already mentioned visible.

While, at the initial stage, social relationship networks cause the establishment of bonds and create the course of action through feelings of

---

trust, this bond of trust might cause obligations and fear after a certain time. This situation reveals itself mostly in the divorces which occur in families established through social networks based on the feeling of trust.

When we consider the importance of the social networks which individuals who came to Germany through marriage migration preferred during the socialising experience or had to interact with, language is important in migration experience and as the tool of interaction in social networks. At this point, the trust networks are the most significant of references in the occurrence of marriages.

> *"I came to Germany in 1999 after getting married. We were introduced through our relative and married in 3 weeks. The intermediary gave the reference. We trusted... "*
>
> *Interviewee 4*

It is observed that the feeling of trust, which is the primary factor for the realisation of the marriage, is provided through social relationship networks. Social networks are again defined according to gender roles in patriarchal societies. In the migration relationship, which is one of the ways to create these networks, social gender roles are determinant. There is a distinct relationship between using social networks and social gender. The conducted studies revealed that women describe themselves in networks to compared men in relatively limited networks. In this context, in social networks where men are present, women take less central and determinant positions. This situation, which is more valid especially in the workplace, affects the networks in more negative ways in the cases where women have little children (Basak and Oztas, 2010: 32). Hence, women are in the disadvantaged group in having social capital reserves and using them. Interviewee 5 explains how she got married through consanguinity relationship networks as follows.

> *"I came after getting married at the age of 18. We met through a relative and our families got along so we decided to marry... "*
>
> *Interviewee 5*

As can be seen from the examples, meeting with the ex-spouse through "acquaintance" and "relative" and "countryman" is defined as the trust bond. Meeting through an acquaintance or relative seems like a better start. This condition takes the shape of bonding after the marriage and hardens the relation between spouses. Interviewee 6 and interviewee 7 state the manner of their marriages like this.

"... I came to Germany by marrying my relative. He was someone we knew..."

Interviewee 6

"... I had an arranged marriage through a friend..."

Interviewee 7

The fundamental reason behind the formation of an arranged type of relationship is the trust felt for the intermediary person. This trust somehow seems like the guarantee of the relationship. There is a strong correlation between marriage migration and social relationship networks. Being an "acquaintance", "relative" or "countryman" seems like the special bases of confidence-building in migrating to an unknown place. In the next phase, these networks are defined by their bonding manner.

When we inspect the definition of reasons for divorce, the *family effect* is defined as the second most significant effect on the 161 people who were studied (Atila Demir, 2010: 172). All of the 8 individuals in our sampling showed the family effect as one of the major reasons in their divorce. This effect is the bond which existed in the process of establishing the relationship network and is structured with the feeling of trust. After a while this bond is surrounded with a feeling of obligation.

"... I met with the Turkish families when I first got here. My husband's family was not here but they would check on him even with the telephone. They used to decide where we should spend our money or where to invest. I didn't have many Turkish friends left after I divorced; the conducted studies revealed that women could manifest themselves in networks compared to men in relatively limited networks.

Interviewee 8

Not being able to go out to a public space is shown as the most significant area where family control is experienced, even for learning a language. Also, language learning is defined as the critical step for an individual to socialise outside and it can be limited. It also provides that transfer of gender roles. Thus the transformation of social gender roles is observed.

> *"...I had too much difficulty because I didn't know the language. I couldn't go out for a long time. My husband's family was always in our place and they intervened in everything. His family is the most important reason for our divorce..."*

Interviewee 4

> *"...there was education and age difference between me and my husband. He was 10 years older than me. And our families didn't get along after we got married. We didn't live together but it felt like they were always with us..."*

Interviewee 5

One of the most important points in the examples that should be noticed is that social networks which had a positive effect in the initial stage of the migration can have a negative effect after the divorce. These networks have been transformed into an obligatory structure after the marriage and the negative effects of social capital become distinct at this point.

Traditional marriage types can be seen as an agreement not only amongst the spouses but also in families. Young and old women are active in managing this process in the marriages which occur through migration due to this awareness (Akpınar, 2007: 342). Hence, in the conditions where problems are experienced, social networks oppress the individual much more severely and surround him or her. One of the basic reasons for this is the limited choices (in every sense, relationship and social) due to being an immigrant. Interviewee 2 states this situation as follows:

> *"...the problem was conflict between families, his family used to judge mine a lot, their constant presence with us suffocated us..."*

Interviewee 2

The negative aspect of social capital might be effective in time within the family structures formed in the host country through social capital tools.

Bonding Social Capital within Social Networks and Gender

Social gender is a concept that defines males and females in a cultural sense and all of the roles built by societies to distinguish the two genders from each other. Explanations regarding femininity and masculinity have been related to sex hormones and biological secretions for many years. There are two main opinions in society to explain the differences between men and women: the "naturalistic" view, which attributes these differences to biological causes, and the "progressive" view which attributes them to social differences built culturally and transferred through generations. These differences begin to be built as soon as the baby is born (or even prior to birth). Baby girls and boys are defined according to their social gender and socialise respectively. Individual, social and institutional factors are determinant in the production of social gender. In this context, arguments regarding gender and social gender have progressed from a biologically-based approach to the current social building approach over the last century (Ecevit et al., 2011: 4-5; Risman and Davis, 2012: 3/11). In the sexist regime, women are defined as responsible for reproduction and men are defined as responsible for production itself. This difference in responsibilities is combined with the biological difference and presented to both genders as if it were natural. Reacting to these situations can of course normally be explained by the interiorising of these gender differences during childhood (Kılıç, 2013: 2). A criticism of masculinity in feminist theory is that women have been defined as "the other" throughout history and placed at the bottom of the gender hierarchy owing to the work they do. For this reason, Simone De Beauvoir defined women, especially in patriarchal societies, as "the other". In other words, a woman is an individual whose existence is only related to a male (Bora, 2012: 10; Pilcher and Whelehan, 2004: 90). As a result of all this, it is known that a social life which is built upon women being passive, compatible and obedient causes invisibility in certain areas of social life. Add to this the fact that the percentage of women who work in politics or at high levels in the working environment compared to men is very low. According to TUIK – the Turkish Statistics Institute – the number of illiterate women was five times greater than the number of illiterate men in 2015. The percentage of women employed was 26.7% and the percentage of female Congress members was 14.7%. This also greatly affects women's personal choices in marriage and family processes and their behaviour.

As Interviewee 1 stated, the pressure caused by intense consanguine relationships and that continues after marriage is shown to be a major factor in the decision to seek a divorce.

> *"...I grew up very easy-going. My husband's family wasn't open to society. I have never met anybody new during 6 years of our marriage. I couldn't step outside the house. They didn't even let me have the house keys. I wouldn't go anywhere without my husband. These problems grew after a while and I decided to get a divorce..."*

Interviewee 1

The desire of an individual to live in better conditions is the basis of migration. This is the common thread that binds all the types of migration. However, at the same time, being an immigrant brings disadvantages and social exclusion through this one particular dimension, whereas being a female immigrant multiplies the difficulties that can be experienced. This situation is observed very clearly in other reasons for migration. The troubles which female immigrants have gone through include not having certain citizenship and social rights due both to being an immigrant and a woman (Dedeoglu and Gokmen, 2011: 1), as in the case of marriage through migration, although the fundamental trust networks are used as tools, the exclusion experienced is magnified. As a result, the problems that may be caused by being an immigrant coupled with social gender inequality are observed afterwards. Being an immigrant sharpens and transforms the social gender inequalities. Interviewee 3 states this condition as follows:

"...why this marriage lasted so many years? Maybe I just did not have the courage... Everybody knows each other here and they are much more conservative, breaking up is not easy... "

Interviewee 3

In some cases, however, being an immigrant might cause the problems caused by social gender to be covered by the immigration related problems.

"...I had lived all the troubles that can be lived by a person who arrives here after making an arranged marriage. The language problem is at first. My husband was very comfortable with foreign women. But he wouldn't let me cross my legs near little boys. His family was in Turkey, he used to send them money constantly. We send money to my husband's family to buy a house for us. They said they bought a villa but it was a single room basement floor flat. My husband didn't protest not to upset his family. I broke up with him when he had an affair. "

Interviewee 8

In some cases, the bonding social networks can become much stronger with their negative dimension. The concepts of "having the courage", "accumulated", "to be suffocated", used here point out that social capital acted in its negative aspect and involved a bonding quality. The results of the study conducted in 2010 (Atila Demir, 172) are such as to confirm the bonding nature of these networks. According to this, the bonding social networks used in the realisation of marriage transform the gender roles and surround the individual. Interviewee 7 and interviewee 5 are examples of an awareness of social gender.

> *"...My ex-husband used to give all he earned to his family. And they were sending all those to their family in Turkey. My husband would take money from his family if ever the need arose. Whatever his family wanted would happen. He let his family extremely oppress me, he never looked after me."*

Interviewee 7:

> *"...According to my husband my duty was to be the house labourer. He didn't send me to a course in case I would learn the language and become shrewd. Even when we went to see a gynaecologist my husband would translate everything. That is really sad ..."*

Interviewee 5

One of the main reasons for the troubles happening in marriages through migration is the problem of not knowing the language. The problems caused by being an immigrant can get much more complex when language inefficiency is added. And when femininity is added to this position, social gender inequalities are reproduced with the sanctions. Gender inequality-based problems are experienced mostly in domestic roles and inter-family relationships. Thus, the social capital networks transform the social gender roles in a bonding and obligatory manner. The social control of women in the external groups to which they migrated through marriage is low. However, in the internal group their social control is felt to be high because it occurs through social networks.

Conclusion

Social capital is a subject for studies mostly for its positive content and effect. Yet, besides that, it is observed that the negative and bonding effects of social capital and relationship networks are considered. This study is conducted to demonstrate how the existing situations in the marriages of individuals who live in Germany and married through social capital and social relationship networks produced downsides of the social capital and caused oppression and exclusion.

By considering the findings of the research performed in the preliminary study and the analysis of the interviews conducted using the purposeful sampling, the examination of how the relationship of marriage established using social capital was reshaped after a while could be performed. It was determined that when social capital begins to act in a negative way it causes the dissolution of established bonds. This negative effect often reveals itself in redirection or oppression and limitations on the behaviour of individuals.

There is no doubt that there are various and intertwined reasons for marriages ending. In fact, it might seem impossible to examine the reasons objectively most of the time. However, the fact that some processes cause common results makes it mandatory to approach these elements. There is a strong correlation between marriage migration and social relationship networks. In this sense, having an acquaintance is a feature which an individual needs, especially during migration. It involves trust within. Being an immigrant causes the individual to feel despair because of being deprived of the social relationship networks previously relied upon and this leads to an attempt to relieve this despair by forming new acquaintances and networks.

Besides, these networks might sometimes assume obligatory and scary shapes in certain conditions. The examples examined in the study are examples of this. When bonding networks become a governing force in the behaviour of actors, conflicts arise and the existing social capital is defined by its negative aspect. In the family structure which is established in the host country through social capital tools, negative aspects of social capital might be effective. This transformation can be seen clearly, especially during the establishment of the marriage and the phases of its termination. The study aims to reveal this transformation.

At the same time, social gender roles become more distinct with their sharp features in these marriages conducted through social networks, and the bonding nature of social networks becomes evident. Women's control over external locations which they migrated to through marriage is low. However, in the internal group, their social control is high because the marriages occurred through social networks. This contradiction both strengthen the negative bonding nature of the social capital and affect the awareness levels of women and causes a transformation in social gender stereotypes. The social relationship networks used on marriage migrations are built upon a trust dependent system. Its transformation in a negative way after the marriage might make the divorce processes much harder.

Studies on immigration and social gender are receiving greater attention, both at the analytical level and methodologically. The social gender phenomenon is a key quality tool in analytical studies. In this study, immigration, social capital and divorce relations are approached within the framework of social gender. There is still plenty of scope for further progress in determining the effects of migration and gender.

References

Akar, D. and Marti, L. (2015). Söylem çözümlemesi. In: *Nitel Araştırma Yöntem, Teknik, Analiz ve Yaklaşımları*. F. N. Seggie and Y. Bayyurt (eds.), Ankara: Anı Publishing Company, pp. 242-252.

Akmehmet Şekerler, S. (2015). Derinlemesine görüşme. In: *Nitel Araştırma Yöntem, Teknik, Analiz ve Yaklaşımları*. F. N. Seggie and Y. Bayyurt (eds.), Ankara: Anı Publishing Company, pp. 186-201.

Akpinar, A. (2007). İsveç'de yaşayan Türk kadınlarının sosyal ilişki ağları, evlilik ve boşanma durumları. In: *Kökler ve Yollar Türkiye'de Göç Süreçleri*, A. Kaya and B. Sahin (eds.), İstanbul: İstanbul Bilgi Universitesi Publishing Company, pp. 335-357.

Atila Demir, S. (2010). *Türk Göçmen Ailelerinde Boşanma*, Unpublished PhD Thesis, Sakarya University, Institute of Social Science, Sakarya.

Atila Demir, S. (2011). Aile ve sosyal sermaye ilişkisi. *New World Sciences Academy Humanities Sciences*, 6 (4): 897-915.

Başak, S. and Öztaş, N. (2010). Güven ağbağları, sosyal sermaye ve toplumsal cinsiyet. *Gazi University Faculty of Economics and Administrative Sciences Journal*, 12 (1): 27-56.

Berger, J. and Mohr, J. (1976). *Yedinci Adam*. C. Capan (translate), İstanbul: Cem Publishing.

Bora, A. (2012). *Kadınların Sınıfı Ücretli Ev Emeği ve Kadın Öznelliğinin İnşası*. İstanbul: Iletisim Publishing Company.

Bourdieu, P. (1986). *The Forms of Capital*. Accessed from https://faculty.georgetown.edu/irvinem/theory/Bourdieu-Forms-of-Capital.pdf.

Castles, S. and Mark, J. M. (2008). *Modern Dünyada Uluslararası Göç Hareketleri*. B. Uğur Bal and I. Akbulut (translate), İstanbul: İstanbul Bilgi University Publishing Company.

Chiswick, B. R. (1999). Are immigrants favourably self-selected? *The American Economic Review*, 89 (2): 181-185.

Christakis, A. N. and Fowler, H. J. (2009). *Sosyal Ağların Şaşırtıcı Gücü ve Yaşantımızı Biçimlendiren Etkisi*. D. Yüksel (translate), İstanbul: Varlık Publishing Company.

Cohen, J. H., and Sirkeci, I. (2011). *Cultures of Migration: The Global Nature of Contemporary Mobility*. Texas: University of Texas Press.

Coleman, S. J. (1988). Social capital in the creation of human capital. *The American Journal of Sociology*, 94: 95-120.

Çelik, H. and Ekşi, H. (2008). Söylem analizi. *Marmara University Educational Science Journal*, 1: 99-117.

Dedeoğlu, S. and Gökmen, C. E. (2011). *Göç ve Sosyal Dışlanma Türkiye'de Yabancı Göçmen Kadınlar*, Ankara: Efil Publishing Company.

Ecevit, Y. et al. (2011). *Toplumsal Cinsiyet Sosyolojisi*. Anadolu University: Eskişehir.

Faist, T. (2003). *Uluslararası Göç ve Ulus Aşırı Toplumsal Alanlar*. İstanbul: Bağlam Publishing Company.

Field J. (2006). *Sosyal Sermaye*. B. Bilgen and B. Sen (translate). İstanbul: İstanbul Universitesi Publishing Company.

Marriage and Divorce

Fukuyama, F. (2001). Social capita, civil society and development. *Third World Quarterly*, 22 (1): 7-20.

Gans, J. H. (1961). Planning and social life: Friendship and neighbour relation in suburban communities. *Journal of the American Planning Association*, 27 (2): 134-140.

Kadushin, C. (2012). *Understanding Social Networks Theories, Concepts, and Findings*, New York: Oxford University Press.

Kastoryano, R. (2000). *Kimlik Pazarlığı Fransa ve Almanya'da Devlet ve Göçmen İlişkileri*. A. Berktay (translate). İstanbul: İletişim Publishing Company.

Kaya, A. and Kentel, F. (2005). *Euro-Türkler Türkiye ile Avrupa Birliği Arasında Köprü mü Engel mi?* İstanbul: İstanbul Bilgi University Publishing Company.

Kilic, A. Z. (2013). *Ebeveynlerin Toplumsal Cinsiyet Algısı ve Çocuk Yetiştirmeye Etkileri*. Research Report, Istanbul Bilgi University, Cocuk Calısmalar, Accessed from file:///C:/Users/sau/Downloads/%C3%A7ocuk%203.pdf

Massey, S. D. and Aysa M. (2005). *Social Capital and International Migration from Latin America*. Expert Group Meeting on International Migration and Development in Latin America and the Caribbean, Mexico City.

Massey, D. S., Arango, J., Hugo, G., Kouaouci, A., Pellegrino, A. and Taylor, J. E. (1993). Theories of international migration: a review and appraisal, *Population and Development Review*, 19: 431-466.

Migrationsbericht des Bundesamtes fur Migration und Fluchtlinge im Auftrag der Bundesregierung, Migrationsbericht (2006). *Bundesministerium des Innern Bundesamt fur Migration und Fluchtlinge*, Germany.

Narayan, D. and Cassidy, M. F. (2001). A dimensional approach to measuring social capital: Development and validation of a social capital inventory, *Current Sociology*, 49 (2): 59-102.

Özgür, E. M. and Aydın, O. (2010). Türkiye'de kadın evlilik Göçü. *e-Journal of New World Sciences Academy*, 5 (1): 18-31.

Özgür, E. M. and Aydın, O. (2011). Türkiye'de evlilik Göçünün mekansal veri analizi teknikleriyle değerlendirilmesi. *Coğrafi Bilimler Dergisi*, 9 (1): 29-40.

Pieterse, J. N. (2003). *Social Capital and Migration, Beyond Ethnic Economies*, USA: Sage Publications, University of Illinois.

Pilcher, J. and Whelehan, I. (2004). *50 Key Conteps in Gender Studies*, London: SAGE Publications.

Putnam, R. D. (1995). Bowling alone: America's declining social capital, *Journal of Democracy*, 6 (1): 65-78.

Risman J. B. and Davis, G. (2012). From sex roles to gender. *2012 Sociopedia.isa*: 1-16

Sirkeci, I. (2003). Migration from Turkey to Germany: An ethnic approach. *New Perspectives on Turkey*, *29*: 189-207.

Sirkeci, I. (2009). Transnational mobility and conflict, *Migration Letters*, 6 (1): 3-14.

Sirkeci, I., Cohen, J. H., and Yazgan, P. (2012). Turkish culture of migration: Flows between Turkey and Germany, Socio-Economic Development and Conflict, *Migration Letters*, 9 (1): 33-46.

Straßburger, G. (2004). Transnational ties of the second generation: Marriages of Turks in Germany. In *Transnational Social Spaces: Agents, Networks and Institutions*, E. Ozveren and T. Faist (eds.), Aldershot: Ashgate, pp. 1-23.

Sunata, U. (2014), Tersine beyin göçünde sosyal ağların rolü: Türkiyeli mühendislerin Almanya'dan geriye göç deneyim ve algıları. *Türk Psikoloji Yazıları*, 17 (34): 85-96.

TUİK (2016). *İstatistiklerle Kadın 2015*, News Journal, No: 21519, 07 March 2016.

Turan, K. (1992). *Almanya'da Türk Olmak, F. Almanya'da Yaşayan II. Kuşak Türklerin Sosyalizasyonu ve Kültür Değişmesi*, İstanbul: Sümer Publishing Company.

Urry, J. (1999). Mekanları Tüketmek, R. G. Ogdul (translate), İstanbul: Ayrıntı Publishing Company.

User, İ. (1996). Evlilik göçü. In *II. Ulusal Sosyoloji Kongresi, Toplum ve Göç*, T.C. State Statistical Institute, Mersin, pp. 556-563.

Woolcock, M. and Narayan, D. (2000). "Social capital: Implications for development theory, research and policy". In *The World Bank Research Observer*, Vol. 15, No. 2 (August 2000), pp. 225-249.

Yazgan, P. (2010). *Danimarka'daki Türkiye Kökenli Göçmenlerin Aidiyet ve Kimlikleri*, Unpublished PhD Thesis, Sakarya University Institute of Social Science, Sakarya.

Yazgan, P. (2016). Hareketlilikte kimlik inşasına yönelik analitik bir çerçeve, *Göç Dergisi*, 3 (2): 282-296.

Chapter Eight

Effects of Refugee Crisis on Gender Policies: Studies on EU and Turkey

Pelin Sönmez

Introduction

Debates on "migration of women" got stronger when globalization and its challenges were felt around 1980 and onwards. In Europe, the period between 1960 and 1973 was known as the golden age of social welfare state while in the 1990s this social welfare model came into a crisis and many European governments cut resources on social services. Suddenly, migrant women began to be a rational choice to compensate the gap as they provided cheap labour for social welfare services. As a result, home care became the most common social welfare service supplemented by migrant women (Öner, 2015: 358). This actually increased the demand for female migrant workers who often come from countries outside Europe. Bisi Adeleye-Fayemi argues from another perspective in her studies and says that the globalization and implementation of economic policies resulted in the feminization of poverty, which actually refers a situation where "women rather than man are especially at risk of being poor in industrialized countries" (Hyndman and Giles, 2011: 363). In the paper titled "Creating a New World with New Visions: African Feminism and Trends in the Global Women's Movement," she points out an important observation about Africa, and says "African women began to be poorer, they began to migrate" (Msila, 2014: 546). By this determination, we are able to see one of the basic causes of the continuous migration flow from Africa to Europe.

Migration of women does not only occur because of economic reasons, but also as a result of a pressures following a war or a kind of violence arising from conflicts such as ethnic, tribal or religious. These women are often classified as refugees and they are, in fact, the most disadvantaged group of migrant women living in host countries. They generally face many difficulties throughout their journey to the host country such as physical violence, abuse and harassment. Then they also face problems while living in the host country in the form of, for example, lack of social integration, segregation, non-recognition of vocational skills and so on. At this point, Doreen Indra is an important figure who draws our attention to women in forced migration and gender issues. Indra says forced migration does not fix unequal gender relations or it does not carry the arguments of current policies and aid agencies activities (Akis, 2015: 383).

It is known that female migrants' participation in labour market is relatively low compared to male counterparts. A research on resettlement expectations of Iraqi refugees living in Lebanon, Jordan and Syria after the Iraqi War, offers a good example for female refugees' exploitation and overqualification[35] in the labour market. It notes that most of the time, those women have to accept jobs that are not commensurate with their professional qualifications or profile; and when they face financial difficulty (e.g. such as receiving no money transfers from Iraq), they unfortunately seek gain illegal employment (Riller, 2009). This actually can be a negative factor for their societal integration, as well. Hence, studies on labour market integration of refugees show that the societal integration is in line with migrants' employment capacity (Barslund et al., 2017: 1, 5). Therefore, integration policies targeting women as one of the most disadvantaged groups should be implemented actively in regions facing forced migration flows. Today, as Europe has continued to be the most attractive destination for forced migration flows from conflict regions of Middle East and Africa, attitudes towards refugee women in Europe and EU policies, in particular, towards refugee women emerge as important, but yet underemphasized, areas to be investigated.

However, since 2011, EU policies have been unsuccessful in engaging with the protection of refugees and fostering social inclusion of refugees produced by the Syrian War. It is often stated that the EU rather concerns about security and invests in border control measures as a reaction to forced migration (Freedman, et. al., 2017: 11). There are some studies on problems, especially in employment, faced by refugee women in host countries and these are discussed in the next section of this chapter.

---

[35] For definitons and debates on overeducation see Johnston et al. (2010), Khattab et al. (2011), Sirkeci et al. (2015).

However, a study carried out by Gerard and Pickering (Gerard and Pickering, 2013: 10) is important here as they interviewed refugee women who were coming from all over Africa and concluded that the EU have failed to materialize on adopting an integrated approach to migration management within a human rights persepctive.

International organizations such as the United Nations (UN), on the other hand, seems to be no better than the EU regarding the protection of refugee women. Sexual harassment towards refugee women has been first discussed at the First United Nations World Conference on Women in 1975. United Nations High Commission for Refugees (UNHCR) also held a World Conference for the Decade on Women in Copenhagen in 1980 and a paper titled with "Refugee Women Status in the World" was presented in the Conference. Proceedings of these conferences show that refugee women were regarded as victims and vulnerable in those years. Moreover, UNHCR first published a guide on protection of refugee women and gender in 1991. The guide was not binding for the member (signatory) states but they were gor guidance. This model was adopted by several countries as well and for example, Canada, Sweden, Australia, USA and England developed their own guidelines for protecting refugees from gender-based disadvantages. Women's Commission for Refugee Women and Children, an independent institution, also prepared a special guide headed "UNHCR Policy on Refugee Women and Guidelines on their Protection" in 2002. However, those guides were generally incapable of finding tangible solutions for the problems faced by refugee women (Akis, 2015:384).

This chapter examines policies and initiatives of the EU and Turkey on refugee women in order to understand the future of integration of Syrian women in Turkey. Here I will question the EU as a model and look into its legal structure and support that specifically targeted towards refugee women. By doing so, I will ask whether the EU may be a model for Turkey, as a candidate country, for refugee women participation in labour market and integration with the host society in general. In the first section of the chapter, I will be presenting a general view on migrant and refugee women status in the labour market by giving examples from Europe, Syria and Turkey. Legislation and initiatives in the EU and Turkey are presented in the second section of the chapter, and the last section of this chapter draws on a specialist survey interviewing 100 Syrian women living in Sultanbeyli district of Istanbul in 2016. The survey results are indicative of employment capacity and social adaptability of those refugee women we interviewed, and these findings could be helpful for possible future policy development in Turkey and at the EU level.

Do migrant and refugee women participate in labour market on different political models?

Gender regime in Turkey has some pre-Islamic and modern qualifications. Savran describes gender in Turkey within a general framework by referring Tillion's work which indicates common gender based practices attributed to Mediterranean basin. Gender here, has pre-Islamic roots and it is shaped with tribal structure that protects purity of ancestry and conquest policies. Islam itself, in fact, created a protective reaction in these societies as it gave the right of succession to the girls. However, Islam became one of the factors in those tribal base communities within the process of urbanization (Savran, 2013: 117). Attitudes toward gender in modern Turkey were set in the early republican period referring to the years 1920 and 1945. Modernization allowed women into social and political spheres and women was instrumental for this "new" and "western" country as defined in Alkan and Çakır's work (Alkan, 2012: 232). Therefore, women had the mission to breed and raise the new generation. In other words, they would be responsible for ideological and cultural (re)production of the nation. Turkey and Syria, two Muslim countries, have a common ground as Islam is not a state religion in their systems. The Syrian constitution guarantees women to participate in political, social, economic and cultural life that specially opens the way for educated and professional women who live in urban areas particularly (Mogadham, 2003: 12). However, Syrian Arab Republic codes on employment has some discriminatory clauses such as Article 73 of Personal Status Law. The Article says married women require the husband's permission for working, which may be an actual cause that negatively affects female labour force participation in Syria. Hence, according to World Bank Gender Statistics Data Bank, female labour force participation within the total labour force was %17.9 in 1990; it decreased in %14 in 2013 and increased slightly to % 15.5 in 2014 (UN Women Entity for Gender Equality and the Empowerment of Women).

The EU, on the other hand, aims to achieve gender equality since Treaty of Rome was signed; and in every founding treaty of the EU, articles on equal pay, equality in employment or combating discrimination are fixed features. Moreover, EU adopts legally binding directives on equal treatment for men and women at work and protection on pregnant workers and rules on access to employment (Directive 2006/54/EC of July 2006, Directive 92/85/EEC of October 1982). The national equality bodies that are found in every member state help control the implementation of EU laws on gender equality. A system based on regular meetings between EU Commission and those equality agencies provide continuous contact among institutions. In sum, the EU has a solid legal ground and commitment for promoting gender equality.

However, according to the studies and observations on the labour market participation of women in the EU, it is worth saying that employment rates of women are generally lower than those for men in all of the member states despite the fact that women are increasingly well qualified and educated year by year. According to the 2014 statistics, EU28 employment rate for men (aged 20-64) was 75% while it reached only 63.5% for women, indicating Malta, Italy, Greece, the Czech Republic, Romania, Slovakia, Poland, Hungary, Luxembourg and Ireland as having large gaps between male and female employment rates (European Commission European Semester Thematic Fiche Labor Market Participation of Women, 2014 Statistics). World Bank data about female labour force participation on country basis shows that Syrian female participation of total labour force was 17.9% in 1990 and it decreased to 15.5% in 2014 (The World Bank Data of Female Labour Force Participation, 2014). In Turkey, labour market participation among women differs throughout modern Turkish history. Statistics shows that, female labour force participation rates before 1950's were above 80%, including the labour force in agricultural sector, but it decreased to 43% in 1980 and to 23% in 2010. One of the major reasons behind this decreasing statistic is the increasing "domestic worker" status since 1950s. The domestic migration from rural to urban, which steadily had risen since 1950s, seclude women that worked mostly in agricultural sectors as unpaid family worker in rural area to their house in urban areas (Alkan and Çakır, 2012: 242).

Migration, employment and gender issues has common grounds such as social inclusion, citizenship, development and they are interconnected. Starting with the correlation between gender and employment, the top issues can be counted as proportionally low participation of women in paid employment, especially in poorer countries; agricultural sector's dominance in women's employment; wage gaps between women and men and deeming women worthy of such areas which are traditionally linked with gender roles (Elias Ferguson, 2010: 235). Citizenship is one of the main topics that relates to migration, employment and gender at the same time. Migrant women's citizenship can be possible from paid work in many cases. First, paid work often is key in enabling migrant women access to social citizenship rights, including the right to stay or to bring over family members. Second, migrant women's access to skilled work is conditional on the degree of their legal inclusion through migration and labour market regulation (Erel, 2009: 79). Since employment issue is closely associated with the migration of women issue, one can claim that migrant women generally work at the bottom of the occupational hierarchy, where most of them work as domestic workers, entertainers, nurses, and factory workers. Migrant women hardly reach at the same earning levels, compared to native born or non-migrants. Denmark is a concrete example concerning this discrimination where non-Western immigrants are disadvantageous on employment probabilities after the year of 1984. A research held in Denmark shows that non-Western women who arrived the country after 1984, have a lower chance for getting white-collar jobs (Brodmann and Polajeva, 2007) which are generally for professional and intermediate class positions that require high skills in the field.

Domestic workers are specially defined vulnerable as many problems such as sexual harassment, rape, non-payment or underpayment of wages, verbal/ physical abuse may occur due to the lack of inspection in private homes (Shamim, et.al., 2014: 233). Yet, it is very popular as a "migrant woman job" in many European countries and in Turkey as well. A typical example explaining the relationship between migrant women employment and home care services was seen in Italy. Women migrants started to migrate to Italy in 1970s in order to make home care services known as a full time "woman job". However, this fact on migration overlaps with increasing participation of Italian women in the labour market. Being a woman migrant is a precondition to enter house work and care services sectors easily. Moreover, Italian migration policies generally supported some migration types to supply house work and care services. In this manner, we can say that even anti-migrant political parties and governments have supported those policies. For example, in 2005 Berlusconi government first created a special quota for 15.000 migrant for doing house work and care services. This quota application has been implemented and also the numbers were increased by governments each year until 2008 (Öner, 2014: 364, 365, 366). Migrant women from Eurasian states and Russia are quite popular at housework jobs in Turkey as well and many of the Turkish employers prefer to employ them as unregistered workers.

Refugees, in general, have barriers arising from communication and language differences. Moreover, being women refugee means facing the inequalities faced by all women, arising from their role as care person and some would argue the continuing resistance to taking women's contribution to the labour market seriously (Dumper, 2002). Therefore, refugees can be defined as the most disadvantageous figures of the immigrant workforce, many of whom may have a traumatic past that negatively affects their integration period. Other factors that cause lesser chance in the labour market can be listed as less access to social networks, facing discrimination by the majority population and risks for being located in areas with poor job opportunities (Manhica, et al., 2015: 195). Moreover, the hosting country - in Scandinavian Countries for example -, only recognizes the professional qualifications of the refugees or asylum seekers with specific trainings done by State representatives itself and those trainings are held in long periods that actually prolongs and therefore negatively affect the employment process of those people. A number of studies from European countries examined refugee women status and those reach conclusions to approve the above-mentioned claims. Starting with a 2015 study held in Sweden, it aimed o examine transition to first employment among specific groups of African migrants and compared to the findings with general population and other immigrants. According to the results, there was an obvious gender gap in transition to first employment and especially male African migrants from Tunisia, Algeria and Egypt were more likely to find employment than females. The study also confirmed refugees' disadvantageous position to transit to first employment and it's said that refugees from Somalia and Ethiopia had lower transition to first employment. The explanation for possible reasons why refugees in Sweden have a lower performance on transition to first employment refers to the introduction program that asylum seekers and their families take to be integrated with the hosting country. This introduction program consists of Swedish language instruction and preparation to insertion into the labour market which possibly is lower employment opportunity (Manhica, et al., 2015: 201). According to these results, introduction programs for refugees should be reconsidered for being more effective.

A separate research from the UK also confirms non-recognition of refugee women qualifications. The survey was held in 2002 to reveal skills and qualifications of refugee women living in London and to examine their utility in the labour market as teachers, doctors and nurses. For the year 2002, unemployment amongst the general population in Britain is estimated to be five percent for women and seven percent for men, however the results are more drastic when talking about unemployment of refugees. For example, a study by the Refugee Council in Britain says that 75-80 percent of refugees are unemployed or underemployed. The research results shows that over two-thirds (68 percent) of respondents were employed in their country of origin while less than a fifth (18 percent) described themselves as employed in the UK and 90 percent saying they would like to practice their chosen profession. As a result, women face restrictions on their employment rights and some refugee women are discriminated while the current system requires them to enter at great cost to themselves, both in emotional effort and financial resources (Dumper, 2002: 11, 27). Another study held by Cangiano (2012: 32) using the EU-Labour Force Survey 2008 statistics shows female migrants experience higher inactivity rates than men in all immigration categories with obvious gaps among asylum seekers. These results show that migrant women have limited means of realizing their individual occupational projects. Thus, as Erel claims, they are continuously struggling for recognition of their qualifications and skills and that makes those women less comparative in labour market (Erel, 2009: 81).

Legislation and initiatives in EU and Turkey

Situation in the EU

Beginning with the EU legislation, there is no specific law or regulation on protecting refugee women and guaranteeing their integration. However, refugee women issue is somehow mentioned in general issues such as international protection, tackling discrimination based on race and gender and trafficking in and exploitation of human beings. Important EU legislations related to the above-mentioned issues can be listed as follows;

- European Parliament Report on Women's Immigration,

- EU Directive on qualification of third-country nationals or stateless persons as beneficiaries of international protection

- Directive 2013/32/EU of the European Parliament and of the Council of 26 June 2013 on common procedures for granting and withdrawing international protection

- Directive 2013/33/EU of the European Parliament and of the Council of 26 June 2013 laying down standards for the reception of applicants for international protection

- EU Parliament Draft Report on the situation of women refugees and asylum seekers in the EU (Sansonetti, 2016: 17).

European Parliament Report on Women's Immigration stresses the lack of proper organized and coordinated European immigration policy. In K. 1. Section of the report, it says the EU policy on development and social cohesion should implement effective reception and integration policies for women immigrants including refugees. Moreover, in K. 37. Section, it gives reference to 1951 Convention relating to the status of refugees and calls EU Member States to enforce policies that ensure the equality of all people, that means while a Member State take any measure against illegal migration, it should act against discrimination at the same time. (European Parliament Report on Women's Immigration: the Role and Place of Immigrant Women in the European Union) Directive 2011/95/EU also refers refugee women as Article 20(3) describes the general rules of international protection, meanwhile it mentions refugee women indirectly by referring to the problems that many of them faces. In this article it is said;

> *Member States shall take into account the specific situation of vulnerable persons such as minors, unaccompanied minors, disabled people, elderly people, pregnant women, single parents with minor children, victims of human trafficking, persons with mental disorders and persons who have been subjected to torture, rape or other serious forms of psychological, physical or sexual violence." Article 30, on the other hand, stresses the access to healthcare services for refugees including pregnant women especially and gender-based violence survivors. They would be like nationals of the Member State that has granted such protection according to Article 30. (Directive 2011/95/EU of the European Parliament and of the Council) Directive 2013/33/EU mentions about the standards for the reception of applicants for international protection. General principles are described in Article 21 under Provisions for Vulnerable Persons and it says Member States shall take into account the specific situation of vulnerable persons such as pregnant women, persons who have been subjected to torture, rape or other serious forms of psychological, physical or sexual violence, such as victims of female genital mutilation, (and so on..) in the national law implementing this Directive." (Directive 2013/33/EU of the European Parliament and of the Council) Article 29 (1) of the Directive gives special responsibilities to staff professionals working with refugees. It says Member States shall take necessary basic training with respect to the needs of both male and female applicants whom can be refugees as well.*

As migration is a very hot topic since forced or irregular migration rates increased due to Syrian war, The EU Parliament made a resolution about women refugees and asylum seekers dated back March 2016. This resolution repeats nearly all measures and criteria mentioned above. However, the difference can be observed about detailed suggestions on integration issue. For example, resolution number 9 calls for targeted measures to ensure the full integration of women refugees and asylum seekers by preventing all forms of exploitation, abuse, violence and trafficking. In resolution no. 53 the Parliament calls on the Member States to develop and implement specific measures to facilitate labour market participation of women refugees and asylum seekers, including language classes, literacy programs, lifelong learning and training; it also calls on the Commission, the Member States and local authorities to guarantee the right of refugee girls to access statutory education; highlights the importance of informal and non-formal education and cultural exchange in involving and empowering young women and girls; stresses the importance of widening access to higher education for women refugees; calls for robust and transparent procedures for recognizing qualifications obtained abroad. However, in number 60, the Parliament burden the responsibility on education, healthcare services, employment and housing access mainly to the hosting society (European Parliament resolution on the situation of women refugees and asylum seekers in the EU). Moreover it is worth saying that Parliament Resolutions, in line with Council Resolutions, are non-binding and they only suggest a political desire on a specific matter and generally the aim is the suggestion of a guideline composing national legislations and practices about this subject. There are basic rules on protection of women refugees as observed in the legal framework mentioned above. However, as the most prominent ones are non-binding legal acts, the EU's unity and solidarity cannot be an issue on supporting participatory measures for refugee or asylum seeker women and yet it cannot be a model for Turkey on integrating women refugees to labour market.

Immigrant integration and the measures to provide it for women is another major issue for the EU since 2004, when the Common Basic Principles for immigrant integration policy was adopted. The close relationship between integration and employment revealed when, employment was selected as one of the core areas of integration according to 2009 Malmö Conference Conclusions. In 2010 Zaragoza meeting, the Ministers agreed on such indicators, known as "Zaragoza Indicators" that are counted as; employment rate, unemployment rate, activity rate, self- employment and over-qualification. The Council also agreed with the Commission to launch a pilot project for evaluating the integration policies and programs. According to employment analysis of the project, low employment rates for immigrant women, was observed. The report of the Commission recommends such labour market programs for low skilled and long-term unemployed immigrants including, especially, women with children and it notes that "a review of the impact of gender equality legislation on immigrant women could lead to policy adaptations" (Huddleston, et.al., 2013: 10, 15). However a Commission Communication dating back to 2016 (COM (2016) 95 final/2) mentions the recent inflow of migrants and refugees to EU countries and it particularly stress to provide immediate needs and integration to the labour market and society. Two months after this Communication was announced, an Action Plan for the Integration of Third-Country Nationals was adopted with a special reference to gender dimension of migration and integration on refugee women. The Plan says labour market inclusion is crucial for integration with host country (COM (2016) 377 final). The recommendations here actually shows us that the integration programs implemented through the EU is not enough to include migrant women to labour market (Barslund, et al., 2017: 8).

EU funding programs, on the other hand, do not directly destined to the integration of female refugees and asylum seekers. Yet some funding programs under 2014-2020 European Multi-annual Financial Framework, include female refugee protection and integration missions. Starting with European Regional Development Fund first, it funds interventions for female refugees and women asylum seekers under the ninth priority for promoting social inclusion, combating poverty and any discrimination. European Social Fund Regulation, on the other hand, calls for measures aimed at addressing women's need and promoting gender equality especially on labour market participation. The Rights, Equality and Citizenship Program 2014-2020, promotes equality between women and men and gender mainstreaming; it aims to prevent violence against children, young people, women and other groups at risk and therefore includes refugee women as well. Development Cooperation Instrument is another funding program that indirectly refers to refugee women integration or protection as it promotes gender equality and women empowerment. Fund for European Aid to the Most Deprived is another component for our target group. This Fund include measures aimed at enhancing gender equality and therefore is somehow relates to refugee women. Lastly, Asylum, Migration and Integration Fund, has been created to take into account, among other priorities, the needs of vulnerable groups, such as women, and to foster gender mainstreaming which relates to refugees as an important constituent in policy making process

(Sansonetti, 2016: 19, 20). Having solid and financially strong instruments actually refers a success for the EU and yet is a good example for Turkey.

Situation in Turkey

2,823,987 Syrian citizens were registered biometrically at the end of 2016, and 1,319,208 of whom were women (% 46 of the total) (Sirkeci, 2017: 142). This eventually increasing number actually indicates the need for urgent policies for integration of women, especially, to the labour market. While Syrian women citizens is the specific area of concern in this chapter, it is primarily worth saying that Syrian citizens cannot be regarded as "refugee", under Turkish law. Turkey adopted 1951 Geneva Convention in 1961 under Law number 359, however Turkey put 2 reservation to it. The first one is the condition of having Turkish roots and the second one is about the condition of "geographical boundaries" that means a person can be regarded as refugee only if she comes from states of European Council. The Law 6458 defines refugee as foreigners who come from Member States of European Council and apply for international protection in Turkey which makes Syrian citizens out of this category. However the Directive for "Temporary Protection" has come into effect on 24 October 2014 and this Directive mostly regulated rights and obligations of Syrian citizens living in Turkey. Persons who are under temporary protection benefit such services as health, education, access to labour market, social aid and translation. Article 29 explains provisions on "access to labour market" and mention about a special Regulation that organizes methods, sectors, provinces or procedures of working permit for the persons who have temporary protection identification document. This Regulation was published by the Official Gazette on January 15, 2016 with number 29594. While examining the articles, it is seen that there is neither a reference to gender issue, nor specifying any rights or support mechanism of occupational skills for women.

Article 48 of Temporary Protection Directive has some special protection clauses on humanitarian occasions including women and children. It says, deterrent and protector measures should be taken immediately for the foreigner women who declare themselves or who found to be victims of violence. Moreover it is also indicated in the Directive that required precautions for the ones who found to be victims of human trafficking would be done accordingly under applicable legislation. Another regulation including women is about family reunification. This Directive opens the way for foreigners living in Turkey to demand for family reunification (Erdoğan, 2015: 99).

Concerning the international cooperation and projects for Syrian citizens including women, Foreign Ministry of Turkey gave permission to limited number of (approx. 10 -12) international NGO's to work with. International organizations and NGO's are forbidden to enter the camps and this damages transparency while, absence of human rights observers at the borders causes lack of information in that area (Öner, 2014: 44). Ministry of Interior Directorate General of Migration Management declared UNHCR, International Organization for Migration (IOM) and International Centre Migration Policy Development (ICMPD) as its shareholders at the international level and bilateral or multilateral projects with those organizations are held in order to protect or integrate refugees, asylum seekers or temporarily protected people. "Helping Victims of Human Trafficking in Turkey" Project is an example of a cooperation between Turkey and IOM. As part of the project, 157 Emergency Help Line was opened to international access as of April 2007 for helping potential victims of human trafficking and since than167 victims were rescued using this line.

Survey results with Syrian women citizens living in Istanbul- Sultanbeyli

Before starting with the results and analysis of the survey, it should be noted that this survey is articulated to the field study of an EU project called "Syr-round the Children" which is implemented under Democracy and Human Rights Grant Scheme Program in Turkey. The survey was held in June 2016 with 100 Syrian women who were randomly selected and have lived in Sultanbeyli-Istanbul, and the reason for selecting this location has two factors. The first one can be defined as the "Istanbul" factor, because Istanbul is the second most crowded city according to Human Rights Watch 2015 statistics explaining Syrian population living in Turkish cities. The second factor can be defined as "Sultanbeyli factor" because this province is in top 4 crowded district of Istanbul in terms of registered Syrian population. I should also remark here that Sultanbeyli is a district where income and education level is quite low and the same tendency is valid for Syrians living there, which can be seen from survey results explained below. In this additional survey, 16 questions were asked to the women in order to make an assessment on their participation in Turkish labour market; their willingness to live in Turkey, an EU country or in Syria and effects of Turkish state policies to the integration of those women to the society that they live in. The questions were open-ended, multiple choice and some are designed on Likert scale. Face-to-face interview method was used via asking the questions to the women and an Arabic translator helped to the pollsters for communication.

Demographical variables are important for explaining target groups' inclination to work or their wish to participate in labour force. The survey's age statistics shows that population is generally composed of "working age" women. Most of the participants can be counted "middle age" as 32.7% of participants are aged between 25 and 35; 26.5% of participants are aged between 36 and 45. However, 20.4% of the population can be called as young females that 14.3% is aged between 20and 24 and 6.1% is aged between 15 and 19. Moreover 8.2% declared their age as 46-55 and lastly 12.2% declared their age between 55 and 60. According to the results, 41% of women declared themselves as primary school graduate while 31% said they were illiterate. % 10 declared that they are literate but never attended to school; 12% declared themselves as secondary school graduate and 6% of the sample is high school or university graduate. Moreover, the survey shows that those women are generally newcomers to Turkey as 64% of them responded "how long have you been living in Turkey" question as "up until one year". Here 34% of respondents declared that they have been staying in Turkey about 2-3 years and only 2% of them said they are staying more than 4 years.

Table 8.1. Demographic Variables- Age of Participants

Cumulative Percent	Valid Percent	Age
6,1	6,1	15-19
20,4	14,3	20-24
53,1	32,7	25-35
79,6	26,5	36-45
87,8	8,2	46-55
100,0	12,2	56-60
	100,0	Total

Two questions were asked to know whether those people would like to live in Turkey or any EU member states in 10 years from now. Answers show that women neither wants to stay in Turkey nor in an EU member states in coming years. 67% of women said they do not want to stay in Turkey and surprisingly, 85% of women said they do not want to stay in an EU country. Therefore as long as the war ends, turning to the homeland is a probable option that can be derived from this question. The answers to this question may also be related with the inefficient EU policies, mentioned in the previous section, regarding the protection and supporting labour participation of those women. However, I should remind that many of respondents migrated to Turkey for about a year; therefore their ideas can change as the period they spent in Turkey prolongs.

A couple of questions were asked for defining the working status of women. However, before giving the statistics, I should note here that, in EU Project's grand survey that is implemented to both male and female Syrian citizens, 97.1% of the population declared males as the ones that take family responsibility and only 2.9% declared females as responsible of their family. This answer actually may show us the paternalistic inclination of this group, hence the survey with women also indicates their low participation to the labour market. 85.7% of women said that they were not working in Syria and 14.3% declared that they were working in Syria. 97.4%, on the other hand, said that they are not working in Turkey while 2.6% said they are currently working in Turkey. All of working women among our sample group said they are working in the textiles sector. The next question was designed as open- ended question and it was formulated as "which job would you like to do in Turkey?". The majority of respondents (88.4%) declared that they would not want to work, 4.2% said they would like to work in textile sector; 2.3% said they would like to be domestic worker while the same amount of women said they wanted to be teacher; 1.2% said they would work as police women, while the same amount of women said they wanted to be coiffeur. If this result is generalizable one within the Syrian women population living in Turkey and the EU, the authorities should concentrate on the basic reasons behind this reluctant attitude of those women and they should find possible "pull factors" to make them participate in the labour market.

All of the participants declared that Turkish state does not support them for their current job or for the job that they desire, therefore they did not respond to the next question about the content of Turkish state support on vocational skills. Whether those women consciously replied to this question or they are not aware of such state/local initiative about supporting vocational skills, this result actually shows the inadequacy of Turkish authorities for taking supportive measures on a gendered base.

The following question is about the general needs in everyday life and women mostly responded as food (34%) and furniture (17% says refrigerator, 18% says sofa suite, 13% says electronic equipment), however 15% of participants replied as "nothing". Answers to this question actually show the economic performance of those women, which indicate one third of the sample can be defined "as poor" because they simply require food.

Table 8.2. General Needs in Everyday Life of Participants

%	What are your basic needs in everyday life?
18	Sofa Suite
17	Refrigerator
8	Washing Machine
34	Food
12	Carpet
12	Oven
6	Cloth
3	Air Condition
4	Wardrobe
4	Fan
5	Bed
6	Furniture
13	Electronic Equipment
3	Kitchen Equipment
3	Gas
15	Nothing
6	Other

Syrian women citizens' integration with Turkey is examined in the remaining part of the survey. The participants replied to the question of "do you have difficulties to communicate with Turkish people?" as 63% "yes" and 37% "no". 88% replied as I have neighbours, 2% replied as I have friends and 10% replied as I have both friends and neighbours to this question. The question in the remaining part of the survey is designed on Likert scale and the results shows that, 32.3% of respondents agree with the statement of "I feel like a stranger here" while 25.3% strongly disagree and 22.2% disagree. 65.7% of respondents disagree with the idea of having Turkish friends/neighbours due to knowing Turkish language and only 13.1% agrees with this idea. On the contrary, 48% of the sample agree with the idea of not having Turkish friends/neighbours due to not knowing Turkish language, which 16.3% strongly agrees, 14.3% disagrees and not sure. 36.1% of respondents agrees with the idea of being happy in Turkey while 32% disagrees with it.

43.9% of total population is not sure about building a future for their families in Turkey and 27.6% disagrees with it while the percentage reaches at 45.5% to the question of building a future for herself in Turkey and 24.2% disagrees with it. The cross analysis for those two questions shows that respondents generally do not face difficulties while communicating Turkish people, yet they are mostly not sure and disagree on building a future for their family in Turkey. Moreover, they are generally not sure and relatively less disagree on building a future for themselves in Turkey, which indicates that those women are tended not to stay or work in Turkey for themselves and relatively more eager to stay here in Turkey when they consider their families.

Figure 8.1. Answers to the "I feel like a stranger here" question

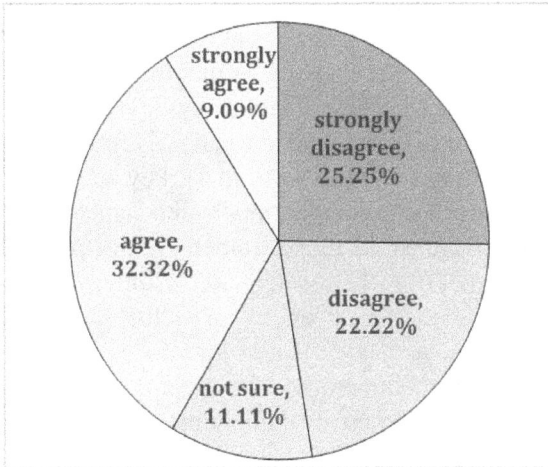

Conclusion

Migration is not a new phenomenon, yet it became a global issue that turns out to be a "problem" for international community since wars, human rights violations, disasters or diseases oblige masses to migrate from one country to another. Migrant women here are facing the same gender problems plus being more disadvantageous in the labour market. Refugee women, on the other hand, are the most vulnerable group with having a traumatic past or facing discrimination problems intensely. They are also disadvantageous in labour market that most of the time their occupational skills are not recognized by the host countries' officials or they generally (have to) work informally.

This chapter examined policies and initiatives towards refugee women in Turkey and the EU in order to make a prediction on their role in labour market. It is clear that the legal framework in Turkey and in the EU have a basis for protecting refugee women while the EU does not refer to them directly in its directives. Yet non-binding resolution and communications of the Parliament and the Commission have addressed women refugees and asylum seekers in the EU since 2016. However, these legal acts of the EU are not sufficient to be a model on protecting and supporting on employment of women refugees for countries like Turkey.

Turkey, meanwhile, tried to manage with the integration of refugees by implementing Temporary Protection Directive after Syrian war, giving no specific reference to women's participation in the labour market. Therefore, although young women escaping from the war in Syria can be a potential for the labour market, the inefficient attitude of Turkey and the EU on protecting and encouraging women refugees in terms of employment seems to negatively affect "domestic worker" status in Turkey or employment problems for the EU. Hence, the survey results from Istanbul-Sultanbeyli district highlighted part of the situation by showing the inclination to "domestic worker" status of refugee women, where most of the respondents implied that they do not want to work in Turkey and all of them declared that the State does not have a support mechanism for enhancing their vocational skills. Besides, as those women are not part of the labour force, it can be a signal for their social exclusion as well, especially in the long term. It is better to keep in mind that defining demographic features of the sample as poorly trained and low income economic status in general may be an imperative for their employment capacity - that most of them neither worked in their home country; nor would like work in the hosting country. This situation, in fact, is a continuous attitude of a specific Syrian women typology explained above, as legal codes and traditions that affect their behaviour in Syria and in Turkey. In this manner, one should explore the complex relationship between behavioural patterns and gender, and concentrate on finding the "pull factors" for those women to provide participation in the labour market.

References

Akis, Y. (2015). "Uluslararası zorunlu göç literatüründe toplumsal cinsiyet: Başlıca yaklaşımlar ve eleştiriler". In S. S. Gülfer- Ihlamur Öner and N. A. Şirin Öner (eds.). *Küreselleşme Çağında Göç- Kavramlar, Tartışmaları*. Istanbul: İletişim Publishers.

Alkan, A. and Çakır, S. (2012). "Osmanlı İmparatorluğu'ndan modern Türkiye'ye cinsiyet rejimi: Süreklilik ve kırılmalar". In F. Alpkaya and B. Duru (eds.). *1920'den Günümüze Türkiye'de Toplumsal Yapı ve Değişim*. Ankara: Phoenix Publishers.

Barslund, M., Di Bartolomeo A. and Ludolph, L. (2017). *Gender Inequality and Integration of Non- EU Migrants in the EU*. CEPS Policy Insights, No. 2017/06.

Brodmann, S. and Polavieja, J. G. (2007). *Immigrants in Denmark: An Analysis of Access to Employment, Class Attainment and Earnings in a High- Skilled Economy*. DemoSoc Working Paper, No. 2007- 21. Accessed from http://www.upf.edu/demosoc/_pdf/DEMOSOC21.pdf on 15 June 2016.

Cangiano, A. (2012). *Immigration Policy and Migrant Labour Market Outcomes in the European Union: New Evidence from the EU Labour Force Survey*. LAB-MIG- GOV (Which Labor Market Governance for a More Dynamic and Inclusive Europe?) Project, FIERI Working Paper. Accessed from http://labmiggov.fieri.it/wp-content/uploads/2012/05/Cangiano-Lab-Mig-Gov-Final-Report-WP4.pdf on 9 March 2017.

COM. (2016). 377 Final Action Plan on the Integration of Third Country Nationals. Brussels, 7. 6. 2016.

COM. (2016). 95 Final/2 2016 European Semester: Assessment of Progress on Structural Reforms, Prevention and Correction of Macroeconomic Imbalances, and Results of In-depth Reviews under Regulation. (EU) No 1176/2011. Brussels, 7. 4. 2016.

Directive. (2011). 2011/95/EU of the European Parliament and of the Council, on Standards for the Qualification of Third-Country Nationals or Stateless Persons as Beneficiaries of International Protection, for a Uniform Status for Refugees or for Persons Eligible for Subsidiary Protection, and for the Content of the Protection Granted. 13.12.2011.

Directive. (2013). 2013/33/EU of the European Parliament and of the Council Laying Down Standards for the Reception of Applicants for International Protection, 26 June 2013.

Directive. (2006). *2006/54/EC of July 2006.* Directive 92/85/EEC of October 1982.

Dumper, H., (2002). Missed opportunities-A Skills Audit of Refugee Women in London from the Teaching, Nursing and Medical Professions. Greater London Authority.

Elias J. and Ferguson, L. (2010). "Production, employment and consumption". In *Gender Matters in Global Politics: A Feminist Introduction to International Relations*. L. J. Shepherd (ed.). New York: Routledge Press.

Erdoğan, M. M. (2015). *Türkiye'deki Suriyeliler Toplumsal Kabul ve Uyum*, İstanbul: İstanbul Bilgi University.

Erel, U. (2009). Migrant Women Transforming Citizenship, Life Stories from Britain and Germany. Farnham: Ashgate Publishers.

European Commission. (2014). *European Semester Thematic Fiche Labor Market Participation of Women.* 2014 statistics, Accessed from http://ec.europa.eu/europe2020/pdf/themes/2015/labour_market_participation_women_20151126.pdf on 08.05.2016.

European Parliament. (2006). European Parliament Report on Women's Immigration: the Role and Place of Immigrant Women in the European Union. (2006/2010(INI)), 27.9.2006.

European Parliament. (2016). European Parliament Resolution on the Situation of Women Refugees and Asylum Seekers in the EU. (2015/2325-INI), Provisional edition, 8 March 2016.

Freedman, J., Kıvılcım, Z. and Özgür Baklacıoğlu, N. (2017). "Introduction: Gender, Migration and Exile". *A Gendered Approach to the Syrian Refugee Crisis*. Z. Kıvılcım and N. ÖzgürBaklacıoğlu (Eds.). New York: Routledge Press.

Gerard, A. and Pickering, S. (2013). Gender, securitization and transit: Refugee women and the journey to the EU. *Journal of Refugee Studies*, 27 (3): 1- 22.

Huddleston, T., Niessen, J. and Tjaden, J. D. (2013). *Using EU Indicators of Immigrant Integration*. Final Report for Directorate-General for Home Affairs, European Commission, Brussels.

Hyndman, J. and Giles, W. (2011). Waiting for what? The feminization of asylum in protracted situations. *Gender, Place and Culture*, 18 (3): 361- 379.

Ihlamur Öner, S. (2015). "Göçün kadınlaşması ve sosyal refah rejiminin dönüşümü: İtalya örneği". In *Küreselleşme Çağında Göç- Kavramlar, Tartışmaları*. S. S. Gülfer- Ihlamur Öner and N. A. Şirin Öner (eds.). Istanbul: İletişim Publishers.

Ihlamur Öner, S. (2014). Türkiye'nin Suriyeli mültecilere yönelik politikası", *Ortadoğu Analiz*, 6 (61).

Johnston, R., Sirkeci, I., Khattab, N., & Modood, T. (2010). Ethno-religious categories and measuring occupational attainment in relation to education in England and Wales: a multilevel analysis. *Environment and planning A*, 42(3), 578-591.

Khattab, N., Johnston, R., Modood, T., & Sirkeci, I. (2011). Economic activity in the South-Asian population in Britain: The impact of ethnicity, religion, and class. *Ethnic and Racial Studies*, 34(9), 1466-1481.

Manhica, H., Östh, J. and Rostila, M. (2015). Dynamics of unemployment duration among African migrants in Sweden: The contribution of specific country of birth and gender on employment success. *Nordic Journal of Migration Research*, 5 (4): 194- 206.

Mogadham, V. M. (2003). *Modernizing Women: Gender and Social Change in the Middle East*, Second Edition, Boulder: Lyenne Rienner Publishers.

Msila, V. (2014). Poor South African migrant women and their children's education: Is there hope after all? *Mediterranean Journal of Social Sciences*, 5 (14): 546- 553.

Riller, F. (2009). *Observations and Recommendations on the Resettlement Expectations of Iraqi Refugees in Lebanon, Jordan and Syria*. Le: International Catholic Migration Commission (ICMC) and UNHCR: The UN Refugee Agency, Lebanon, Accessed from http://reliefweb.int/sites/reliefweb.int/ files/resources/ DECA0503B94F3301492575EE001978F8-Full_Report.pdf on 7 March 2017.

Sansonetti, S. (2016). *Female Refugees and Asylum Seekers: The Issue of Integration*. European Parliament Directorate-General for Internal Policies Policy Department C: Citizens' Rights and Constitutional Affairs, Brussels.

Savran, G. A. (2013). *Beden, Emek, Tarih: Diyalektik bir Feminizm İçin*. İstanbul: Kanat Publishing.

Shamim, F., Tazeen, N. and Qaseem, N. (2014). Labor migration and gender empowerment: A case study of housemaids. *Asian Social Science*, 10 (3): 232-241.

Sirkeci, I. (2017). Turkey's refugees, Syrians and refugees from Turkey: a country of insecurity. *Migration Letters*, 14(1):127-144.

Sirkeci, I., Acik, N., & Saunders, B. (2014). Discriminatory labour market experiences of A8 national high skilled workers in the UK. *Border Crossing*, 4(1-2), 17-31.

T.C. Ministry of Interior Directorate General of Migration Management. (2015). *Türkiye Göç Raporu.* Ankara, April- 2016.

UN. (2016). *Women Entity for Gender Equality and the Empowerment of Women.* Spring Forward for Women Programme, Syria. Accessed from http://spring-forward.unwomen.org/en/countries/syria on 15 June 2016.

Index

www.ingramcontent.com/pod-product-compliance
Lightning Source LLC
Chambersburg PA
CBHW050221270326
41914CB00003BA/510